Building a High/Scope Program

Head Start Preschool Programs

Building a High/Scope Program

Head Start Preschool Programs

Karen "Kay" Rush

with Tricia S. Kruse

Ypsilanti, Michigan

Published by

High/Scope® Press

A division of the High/Scope Educational Research Foundation

600 North River Street

Ypsilanti, Michigan 48198-2898

(734)485-2000, fax (734)485-0704

press@highscope.org

www.highscope.org

High/Scope Press Editor: Marcella Weiner

Cover design, text design, and production: Judy Seling of Seling Design

Photography:

Betsy Evans — 23

Gregory Fox — Cover (front and back), 1, 7, 9, 10, 13, 14, 19, 20, 27, 28, 29, 31, 37, 41, 42, 47, 48, 49, 50, 55, 57, 58, 61

Lorraine Havard — 21

High/Scope Staff — 5, 17, 24, 25, 32, 33, 35, 39, 52, 53, 56, 62, 116

Library of Congress Cataloging-in-Publication Data

Building a High/Scope program : Head Start preschool programs / Karen "Kay" Rush with Tricia S. Kruse.

    p. cm.

 Includes bibliographical references and index.

  ISBN 978-1-57379-268-4 (soft cover : alk. paper) 1. Education, Preschool. 2. Curriculum planning. 3. Head Start Program (U.S.) I. Rush, Karen, 1961- II. Kruse, Tricia S., 1973- III. High/Scope Educational Research Foundation.

  LB1140.2.B84 2008

  372.21--dc22

2007050247

Printed in the United States of America

10 9 8 7 6 5 4 3 2 1

Contents

Acknowledgments

Working for the High/Scope Educational Research Foundation has been a dream come true for me, and I have enjoyed every assignment I've taken on. This assignment of completing my first book could not have happened without the help and guidance of my fellow beloved coworkers. For the wealth of knowledge from the High/Scope Early Childhood Department, including Ann Epstein, Beth Marshall, Mary Hohmann, Polly Neil, Shannon Lockhart, and Sue Gainsley, thank you so much for your feedback, suggestions, and approval in writing this book. To my editors, Marcella Weiner and Nancy Brickman, thank you for your patience with this first-time author and your expertise in how to "just get it done."

I would not have been able to get this done without the diligent Head Start community whom I love so much. Thanks goes to the staff at The Order of the Fishermen Ministry Head Start, in Detroit, Michigan, in particular to Ms. Janice Hill, who beautifully graces the cover of this book, and Ms. Lorraine Havard, for their input and detailed information and for their vast knowledge of mixing the High/Scope Curriculum with Head Start, which has helped me immensely. To Mrs. Betty Carrol and Mrs. Kori Nieman of Adrian Head Start Comstock Center, in

Adrian, Michigan, thank you for providing me with insight on your special practices in caring for your Head Start preschoolers. To Ms. Patricia James, a.k.a. "the collaboration expert," thank you for your input and insight on the history of the collaboration process. To the staff at Wayne County Head Start, in Westland, Michigan, especially Mrs. Mylon Reynolds, thank you for making sure that your teaching staff is trained in this curriculum that you so fondly believe in. To Ms. Diane Perryman of Southeast Children & Families Development Head Start in Detroit, thank you for our long, deep conversations about the compatibility of High/Scope and Head Start and for allowing me to bounce ideas off of you that ended up in this book. To my former Head Start directors, Ms. Dorothy Davis, Mr. Willie Downer, Mrs. Joan Scales, and Ms. Addie Harrison, thank you for believing in me during every step of my Head Start journey from child recruiter to assistant teacher to teacher to center administrator to assistant education coordinator to education coordinator. I could not have completed this book without the knowledge and experience you've imparted on me while working for and with you.

To my family: My husband, Tommie, your love and support while writing this book was very much appreciated. To my eldest son Marlon Rashad Cox, thank you for following your dreams and sticking to your plan of becoming a NASA aerospace engineer so I can continue to use your story as an example of a Head Start and High/Scope student whose plan-do-review process lives on today. To my daughter SharRon Ariel Rush, thank you for pursuing your dream of becoming a pediatric nurse so I can continue to also reference you as a former Head Start child who knows what she wants. To my second oldest son Tommie IV, thank you for being you and for fathering Lil' Tommie V, so we may enjoy the journey of love and education through plan-do-review all over again.

— Kay Rush
Early Childhood Specialist, High/Scope

Preface

Head Start, a federally funded comprehensive child development program, has served children from economically disadvantaged backgrounds and their families since 1965. It consists of two programs: Head Start and Early Head Start. Head Start serves children three to five years of age and their families. Established in 1994, Early Head Start provides services to low-income children prenatal to age three and to low-income pregnant women. In some regions, there is even Migrant Head Start and American Indian-Alaska Native Head Start for children (up to age five) of migrant and seasonal workers.

The services of Head Start are intended to prepare children to enter kindergarten and to improve the conditions necessary for their success in school and life by enhancing their social and cognitive development. Head Start also offers individualized nutrition and health, education, and social services to the children and their families in its programs. Today nearly 1 million children across the United States participate in Head Start programs (U.S. Department of Health and Human Services [DHHS], 2007a).

Children and families defined as low-income under U.S. federal guidelines (earning income at or below the federal poverty level) are eligible for enrollment in Head Start. Head Start also serves children with disabilities and special needs, children in foster care, and some children from families whose income is over the federal poverty level (e.g., children from families receiving public assistance). Ten percent of each Head Start program's enrollment must consist of children with special needs and disabilities, and no more than 10 percent of all children enrolled may be from families with incomes above the federal poverty level. All Head Start programs have a formal process for recruitment, selection, and enrollment.

Head Start programs can be found in cities, small towns, and rural areas throughout the United States. In fiscal year 2006, there were 1,604 grantees that operated close to 19,000 Head Start and Early Head Start centers and more than 50,000 Head Start classrooms throughout the United States. The children in these centers and classrooms come from different racial and ethnic backgrounds. In fiscal year 2006, Head Start children came from the following backgrounds:

▼ 40 percent Caucasian
▼ 34 percent Hispanic/Latino
▼ 31 percent African American

▼ 6 percent biracial or multiracial

▼ 5 percent American Indian, Alaska Native, Asian Native, or Hawaiian or Pacific Islander

▼ 2 percent Asian (DHHS, 2007a)

In an effort to provide meaningful, developmentally appropriate experiences to the children in these classrooms, many Head Start programs implement the High/Scope Curriculum. In doing so, practitioners reaffirm High/Scope Curriculum's effectiveness and adaptability, regardless of the particular classroom setting, the community in which a program is located, or the population it serves. However, many questions arise from those "in the trenches" as to how to implement and adapt certain aspects of the High/Scope approach to their particular setting while adhering to the Head Start Program Performance Standards by which they are governed and mandated by.

High/Scope and Head Start Works: Research on Effectiveness

Head Start and High/Scope share a long history of providing high-quality services to children at risk of school failure. The emerging body of research in the early 1960s about the effects of environment (not just heredity) on intellectual performance spurred both the High/Scope Perry Preschool Study, which began in 1962, and the creation of Head Start, which began in 1965. As the positive results of the High/Scope research became known, the findings were used to support the reauthorization of Head Start at key points in the program's history. Today it is estimated that one fifth of Head Start programs use the High/Scope Curriculum in their preschool classrooms. The Foundation is also a member of the Head Start Quality Research Center consortium, whose mission

---

Head Start History: A Timeline

1965   As part of President Lyndon Johnson's War on Poverty, the Office of Economic Opportunity launches Project Head Start as an eight-week summer program.

1969   The Nixon administration transfers Head Start to the Office of Child Development in the Department of Health, Education and Welfare. (Today it is a program within the Administration for Children and Families in the U.S. Department of Health and Human Services.)

1972   The Economic Opportunity Act is amended and mandates that at least 10 percent of the national Head Start enrollment consist of children with special needs.

1973   Head Start is expanded to include home-based programs.

1975   Head Start Program Performance Standards are issued.

1994   Inception of Early Head Start, which provides services for children birth to age three and pregnant women.

1998   Head Start Reauthorization Act includes a mandate to expand Head Start to full-day, full-year services.

2007   In November, Congress approved the second reauthorization of Head Start, allotting more money for teacher training.

Sources: DHHS (2007a); Glod (2007); Zigler and Muenchow (1992).

> To obtain the most recent research about Head Start, see the Annotated Bibliography of Head Start Research, a searchable database that includes abstracts of quantitative and qualitative research from 1965 on, at the Office of Head Start Web site.

is to support the improvement of Head Start so that it can continue to enhance the school readiness of the children it serves.

High/Scope has, for many years, conducted research on the effectiveness of Head Start and how to further enhance the program through professional development activities. The High/Scope active participatory learning approach has continued to show positive outcomes for children and their families. Our work with Head Start agencies employing the High/Scope Curriculum in their programs, together with our own research studies, has reinforced our belief in the efficacy of the principles on which the curriculum is based.

More than 40 years of research shows that High/Scope programs advance the development of children and improve their chance of living a better life into adulthood. National research with children from different backgrounds has shown that those who attend High/Scope programs score higher on measures of development than do children enrolled in other preschool and child care programs.

The Foundation is perhaps best known for the High/Scope Perry Preschool Study, comparing children from economically disadvantaged backgrounds who attended the High/Scope program with those who did not. As adults, preschool participants had higher high school graduation rates, higher monthly earnings, less use of welfare, and fewer arrests than those who did not attend the program.

Findings show that for every dollar invested in high-quality early childhood education, the economic return to society saves $16.* This figure includes increased earnings for participants, tax revenues on these earnings, and savings to society in the cost of special education, public assistance, unemployment benefits, and crime (Schweinhart et al., 2005).

Research also shows that Head Start provides an economic return. In a study of Chicago Head Start programs, a follow-up survey of 1,539 twenty-year-olds, two thirds of whom attended Head Start at ages three and four, resulted in these findings: Program participants achieved a higher rate of high school completion (50 percent vs. 39 percent) and lower rate of juvenile arrests (17 percent vs. 25 percent). The program provided an economic return of $7.10 per dollar invested (Reynolds, Temple, Robertson, & Mann, 2001). This research supports the findings of the economic analysis of the High/Scope Perry Preschool Study, adding confidence to the conclusion that an investment in Head Start, and particularly in Head Start programs that use High/Scope, provides significant benefits to participants and society as a whole.

Meeting Accountability Standards

Additional research by independent investigators also demonstrates that High/Scope can help Head Start programs meet demands for accountability in children's learning. Most notably, the Head Start Family and Child Experiences Survey (FACES) found that children in programs using High/Scope, compared to other curriculum models, performed better on selected measures of literacy and social development (Zill et al., 2003). Moreover, alignments show the compatibility between High/Scope and Head Start curriculum requirements (Epstein, 2006). Scores on

---

*Based on constant 2000 dollars, discounted at three percent.

the Child Observation Record (High/Scope Educational Research Foundation [High/Scope], 2003a) can be converted to the Head Start Child Outcomes, and the Preschool Program Quality Assessment (High/Scope, 2003b) has been aligned with the Head Start Program Performance Standards for program accountability (see Appendix D for additional information).

Further, an outgrowth of the High/Scope Curriculum, the Growing Readers Early Literacy Curriculum (GRC; High/Scope, 2005), has proven effective in preparing children to meet accountability standards encompassed by federal No Child Left Behind legislation. These literacy goals are also consistent with the Head Start Child Outcomes Framework (DHHS, 2003). A pilot sample of children, including many from Head Start programs, who in 2003 participated in the GRC and were given the Early Literacy Skills Assessment (ELSA), showed significant gains in the following four curriculum areas around which the GRC is structured: comprehension, phonological awareness, alphabetic principle, and concepts about print (High/Scope, 2004). (For more on meeting Head Start accountability standards with High/Scope literacy materials, see Connecting Head Start Content Areas and Child Outcomes With the High/Scope Curriculum in Chapter 2.)

As the push for school readiness and academics continues to head toward the preschool levels, it is important for adults to remember several things. First, *active participatory learning* — having direct experiences with people, materials, and ideas, and a chance to derive meaning from these experiences through reflection — helps young chil-

dren construct knowledge to make sense of the world. Second, in order for children to be ready to learn, they must first feel safe, secure, and confident in their surroundings and with those who care for them. Positive adult-child interactions, an environment that supports active participatory learning, and a predictable but flexible daily routine support children emotionally, physically, and intellectually. These elements are at the heart of the High/Scope Curriculum and High/Scope's child-centered, active participatory learning approach.

Using High/Scope in the Head Start Preschool Classroom

This book was written from the vast experiences of the author, Karen "Kay" Rush, who has been part of the Head Start community for 22 years, first as a classroom teacher who used the High/Scope Curriculum and then as a Head Start administrator who trained and mentored staff in the High/Scope Curriculum. She currently is an Early Childhood Specialist at the High/Scope Educational Research Foundation. This book addresses those ideas that question the compatibility of Head Start and High/Scope and will diminish the many misconceptions about how the two programs cannot coexist in the same program.

In the Introduction to this book, you will find an overview of the High/Scope approach, which will give you a context for fostering these important principles in your Head Start program. The remainder of the book then provides strategies for building a High/Scope program to best meet the needs of the children you serve in your particular Head Start setting.

1

Introduction: About This Book, About the High/Scope Approach

This book is designed for you — an adult who is implementing the High/Scope Curriculum in a Head Start classroom or center. Adults working in Head Start programs have a tremendous responsibility. In addition to organizing materials and learning spaces and planning activities that build on children's interests, they must make sure children's basic physical and emotional needs are met and are required to complete additional paperwork for each Head Start component as described later in this chapter.

You may already find yourself confronted with a number of issues: Just how do you plan your daily schedule to include children's self-care routines and mealtimes? How do you work with children who have special needs and come to your class with an Individualized Education Program (IEP)? How can you include all of the components and content areas that Head Start requires throughout the day? How do you stay in compliance with the Head Start

Program Performance Standards, meet the mandated Head Start Child Outcomes, and incorporate the High/Scope Curriculum? How do you balance the day and still allow time for teachers to plan together and communicate with parents? This book will help you find answers to these and other questions by presenting anecdotes, strategies, tips, and information on additional resources from teachers in established Head Start programs who are successfully using the High/Scope Curriculum while providing quality care to their children and families.

This book addresses Head Start programs that serve preschoolers in a variety of settings. Some of the other books in the *Building a High/Scope Program* series focus on full-day programs, infant and toddler programs, family child care programs, and multicultural programs, all of which can be a setting for a Head Start program. (See High/Scope's online store at *www.highscope.org* for materials available in the *Building a High/Scope Program* series.)

Issues for Head Start Preschool Programs

You and your colleagues may encounter various challenges and opportunities in working with children who come from a variety of backgrounds with different needs while adhering to Head Start's program standards. The following issues are addressed throughout this book:

Challenges
- Incorporating children's self-care routines and mealtimes into your classroom's daily routines
- Meeting the needs of children from economically disadvantaged backgrounds, children who are English language learners, and children with special needs
- Including all the components and content areas that Head Start requires throughout each day
- Involving families and the community in your program

Opportunities
- Using children's self-care routines and mealtimes as learning opportunities
- Expanding adults' own views of what it means to teach (and reach) *all* children
- Fitting in the Head Start content areas with the daily routine and through open-ended materials in the classroom
- Building stronger families and communities, and having families reinforce at home what you do in the classroom

Each type of Head Start setting provides special challenges. Many issues in Head Start programs center on the daily routine — a major framework of the High/Scope Curriculum. The daily routine provides a consistent but flexible structure to the day, which supports children as they pursue their interests and solve problems.

Whether you work in a Head Start preschool center or family child care program, full- or half-day program, or in a rural or urban setting, this book will help you incorporate the High/Scope active participatory learning approach into your particular setting.

Building Your Program

It takes time to implement the High/Scope approach in a typical child care environment. This is not because the curriculum is difficult to learn or implement, or because it requires expensive materials, but because High/Scope is a *comprehensive approach.* From room arrangement to assessment, from literacy development to conflict resolution, High/Scope meets the needs of any early

childhood program, including the diverse Head Start program settings. You are likely to achieve the best results if you focus on implementing each area well, rather than striving for full implementation in the shortest amount of time.

By following the guidelines for implementing High/Scope in Head Start programs outlined in this book, you will see improvements every step of the way, from planning the scope of your program to participating in a program quality assessment.

Using this book. In order to build a Head Start program based on the High/Scope approach, you will need an understanding of basic High/Scope principles. The remainder of this Introduction provides a brief overview of the High/Scope Curriculum, presenting a review of the curriculum's philosophy, daily routine, guidelines for room arrangement, key developmental indicators, team approach, and recommended observation and assessment tools. These principles are discussed fully in the High/Scope preschool manual *Educating Young Children: Active Learning Practices for Preschool and Child Care Programs* by Mary

Benefits of High/Scope to Head Start Preschool Programs

- Promotes an active learning approach so that *all* children can have meaningful, developmentally appropriate experiences
- Is adaptable to a variety of settings, whether it is a full- or half-day program; is in a rural or urban environment; or is located in a school, home, or center
- Helps Head Start programs meet the demands for accountability in children's learning
- Supports and fosters positive adult-child interactions
- Provides a structure within which children can make choices and follow their interests (the *daily routine*), giving them the sense of security they need to make choices and take risks

Hohmann, David P. Weikart, and Ann Epstein (High/Scope Press, 2008) and in *Essentials of Active Learning in Preschool: Getting to Know the High/Scope Curriculum* by Ann Epstein (High/Scope Press, 2007).

In Chapter 2 we will look at the specific challenges of Head Start program implementation, including integrating Head Start components, positive transitions, and other concerns related to the daily routine, as well as making Head Start and High Scope work together in the same program. In Chapter 3 you will have the opportunity to review sample daily routine schedules for Head Start programs that use the High/Scope Curriculum successfully. In Chapter 4 you will find a series of questions and answers in response to specific challenges Head Start professionals have encountered in their programs that are using the High/Scope Curriculum.

Step-by-step implementation. You are already taking the first big step in implementing High/Scope in your program by picking up this book — read on! Review the step-by-step implementation guide in Appendix A for further help in building your High/Scope program. A reproducible program implementation form and other sample forms are included in this appendix to help you plan. Additionally, Appendix B includes a guide to High/Scope resources for more information on particular topics. Appendix C provides the Head Start Child Outcomes Framework, and Appendix D offers information and charts on how Head Start and High/Scope aligns certain aspects of each program, such as the Head Start Child Outcome Elements and Indicators and the Child Observation Record (COR) as well as the Head Start Program Performance Standards (HSPPS) and the Preschool Program Quality Assessment (PQA).

Overview of the High/Scope Educational Approach*

High/Scope is an "active participatory learning" educational approach to teaching and learning. Active participatory learners have direct, hands-on experiences with people, objects, and events that encourage them to think, imagine, and problem-solve. They construct an understanding of their world and the people around them as they make choices based on their intents and follow through on their plans and decisions while adults offer physical, emotional, and intellectual support. In active participatory learning settings, adults support and gently challenge children's thinking with diverse materials, thoughtful conversations, and nurturing interactions.

Essential principles and guidelines of the High/Scope approach are summarized in the diagram on page 4 in the High/Scope Preschool Wheel of Learning.

---

*Portions of this section are reprinted from *High/Scope ReSource, A Magazine for Educators,* Spring, 2003, Vol. 22, No. 1, pp. 5–7.

The High/Scope Preschool Wheel of Learning

ASSESSMENT
- Teamwork
- Daily Anecdotal Notes
- Daily Planning
- Child Assessment

ADULT-CHILD INTERACTION
- Interaction Strategies
- Encouragement
- Problem-Solving Approach to Conflict

ACTIVE LEARNING
Initiative
Key Developmental Indicators

DAILY ROUTINE
- Plan-Do-Review
- Small-Group Time
- Large-Group Times

LEARNING ENVIRONMENT
- Areas
- Materials
- Storage

Active participatory learning is defined by the following five ingredients:

Materials
Programs offer abundant supplies of diverse, age-appropriate materials. Materials are appealing to all the senses and are open ended — that is, they lend themselves to being used in a variety of ways and help expand children's experiences and stimulate their thought.

Manipulation
Children handle, examine, combine, and transform materials and ideas. They make discoveries through direct hands-on and "minds-on" contact with these resources.

Choice
Children choose materials and play partners, change and build on their play ideas, and plan activities according to their interests and needs.

Child language and thought
Children describe what they are doing and understanding. They communicate verbally and nonverbally as they think about their actions and modify their thinking to take new learning into account.

Adult scaffolding
"Scaffolding" means adults support children's current level of thinking and challenge them to advance to the next stage. In this way, adults help children gain knowledge and develop creative problem-solving skills.

Active participatory learners have hands-on experiences that enable them to construct their own understanding of their surroundings.

High/Scope also offers an age-appropriate approach for infants and toddlers based on the same philosophical principles as its pre-school curriculum. If you work with an Early Head Start (infants and toddlers) program, you may wish to see another book in this series — *Building a High/Scope Program: Infant-Toddler Programs* by Tricia S. Kruse (High/Scope Press, 2005) and *Tender Care and Early Learning: Supporting Infants and Toddlers in Child Care Settings* by Jacalyn Post and Mary Hohmann (High/Scope Press, 2000).

How High/Scope Differs From Other Early Childhood Programs

The High/Scope Curriculum is consistent with the best practices recommended by the National Association for the Education of Young Children (NAEYC), HSPPS, and other guidelines for developmentally based programs. Within this broad framework, however, High/Scope has unique features that distinguish it from other early childhood programs. One is the daily plan-do-review sequence. Research shows that planning and reviewing are the two components of the program day most positively and significantly associated with children's scores on measures of developmental progress (Epstein, 1993).

A second distinctive feature are the key developmental indicators (KDIs) that provide the content of children's learning. These are the building blocks of thinking and reasoning at each stage of development. The 58 preschool KDIs are organized into five major content areas and four subcategories. They include

▼ Approaches to learning

▼ Language, literacy, and communication

▼ Social and emotional development

High/Scope Preschool Curriculum Content

Approaches to Learning
- Making and expressing choices, plans, and decisions
- Solving problems encountered in play

Language, Literacy, and Communication
- Talking with others about personally meaningful experiences
- Describing objects, events, and relations
- Having fun with language: listening to stories and poems, making up stories and rhymes
- Writing in various ways: drawing, scribbling, and using letterlike forms, invented spelling, and conventional forms
- Reading in various ways: reading storybooks, signs and symbols, and one's own writing
- Dictating stories

Social and Emotional Development
- Taking care of one's own needs
- Expressing feelings in words
- Building relationships with children and adults
- Creating and experiencing collaborative play
- Dealing with social conflict

Physical Development, Health, and Well-Being
- Moving in nonlocomotor ways (anchored movement: bending, twisting, rocking, swinging one's arms)
- Moving in locomotor ways (nonanchored movement: running, jumping, hopping, skipping, marching, climbing)
- Moving with objects
- Expressing creativity in movement
- Describing movement
- Acting upon movement directions
- Feeling and expressing steady beat
- Moving in sequences to a common beat

Arts and Sciences
Mathematics
Seriation
- Comparing attributes (longer/shorter, bigger/smaller)
- Arranging several things one after another in a series or pattern and describing the relationships (big/bigger/biggest, red/blue/red/blue)
- Fitting one ordered set of objects to another through trial and error (small cup and small saucer; medium cup and medium saucer; big cup and big saucer)

Number
- Comparing the numbers of things in two sets to determine "more," "fewer," "same number"
- Arranging two sets of objects in one-to-one correspondence
- Counting objects

Space
- Filling and emptying
- Fitting things together and taking them apart
- Changing the shape and arrangement of objects (wrapping, twisting, stretching, stacking, enclosing)
- Observing people, places, and things from different spatial viewpoints
- Experiencing and describing positions, directions, and distances in the play space, building, and neighborhood
- Interpreting spatial relations in drawings, pictures, and photographs

Science and Technology
Classification
- Recognizing objects by sight, sound, touch, taste, and smell
- Exploring and describing similarities, differences, and the attributes of things
- Distinguishing and describing shapes
- Sorting and matching
- Using and describing something in several ways

- Holding more than one attribute in mind at a time
- Distinguishing between "some" and "all"
- Describing characteristics something does not possess or what class it does not belong to

Time
- Starting and stopping an action on signal
- Experiencing and describing rates of movement
- Experiencing and comparing time intervals
- Anticipating, remembering, and describing sequences of events

Social Studies
- Participating in group routines
- Being sensitive to the feelings, interests, and needs of others

The Arts
Visual Art
- Relating models, pictures, and photographs to real places and things
- Making models out of clay, blocks, and other materials
- Drawing and painting

Dramatic Art
- Imitating actions and sounds
- Pretending and role playing

Music
- Moving to music
- Exploring and identifying sounds
- Exploring the singing voice
- Developing melody
- Singing songs
- Playing simple musical instruments

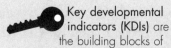 **Key developmental indicators (KDIs)** are the building blocks of thinking and reasoning at each stage of development. High/Scope identifies 58 preschool KDIs organized under five content areas.

In the High/Scope learning approach, adults carefully plan activities that build on and extend children's interests.

▼ Physical development, health, and well-being

▼ Arts and sciences
  – Mathematics
  – Science and technology
  – Social studies
  – The arts

See page 6 for a detailed list of the preschool KDIs.

Adults in High/Scope programs keep the KDIs in mind when they set up the environment and plan activities to encourage learning and social interaction. In addition, High/Scope's preschool child assessment tool — the Child Observation Record (COR) — is based on the KDIs.

High/Scope's Goals for Young Children

High/Scope is a comprehensive curriculum that strives to help children develop in all areas. Goals include helping young children to

▼ Learn through active involvement with people, materials, events, and ideas.

▼ Become independent, responsible, and confident — ready for school and ready for life.

▼ Learn to plan many of their own activities, carry them out, and talk with others about what they have done and what they have learned.

To help them gain knowledge and skills in important academic, social, and physical areas, High/Scope provides children with carefully planned experiences, for example, ensuring that early learning activities and staff development in the area of literacy are compatible with the latest findings from research and practice. The KDIs and recently published curriculum activities in mathematics are aligned with the early childhood standards of the National Council for Teachers of Mathematics. High/Scope teachers are trained to support children in making decisions and solving problems throughout the daily routine, and studies continually demonstrate that children in High/Scope settings show high levels of initiative (Epstein, 1993; Schweinhart et al., 2005). Classroom adults further support social development by helping children learn how to resolve interpersonal conflicts. The National Institute of Child Health and Human Development stresses that all these areas of academic and socioemotional growth are essential for school readiness.

Who Uses High/Scope?

The High/Scope Curriculum serves the full range of children and families from all social, economic, and ethnic backgrounds. It is used in public and private agencies, half- and full-day preschools, Head Start programs, public school prekindergarten programs, child care centers, home-based child care programs, and programs for children with special needs. The High/Scope Curriculum for grades K–5 is used in schools around the country and is approved as a Comprehensive School Reform model. High/Scope's summer residential program for teens, the Institute for IDEAS, was one of the few out-of-school programs recog-

nized by the Program Effectiveness Panel of the U.S. Department of Education.

In addition to the programs throughout the United States using High/Scope, and High/Scope teacher education centers in Canada and South Africa, High/Scope Institutes operate in Great Britain, Indonesia, Ireland, Mexico, The Netherlands, Singapore, and South Korea. High/Scope reaches between 6,000 and 7,000 educators each year with its training programs. High/Scope curricula, assessments, and evaluation tools may be used by High/Scope certified programs as well as others that do not follow the High/Scope approach. For more information on these tools, see the High/Scope Web site at *www.highscope.org*.

Adult-Child Interactions

In High/Scope programs, adults are as active in the learning process as children. A mutual give-and-take relationship exists in which both participate as leaders and followers, speakers and listeners. Adults interact with children by sharing control with them, focusing on their strengths, forming genuine relationships with them, supporting their play ideas, and helping

---

Six Steps to Conflict Resolution

1. Approach calmly.
   — Place yourself at the child's level.
   — Use a calm voice and gentle touch.
2. Acknowledge children's feelings.
   — Name and describe the children's feelings.
   — Avoid asking questions until children are calmer.
3. Gather information.
   — Ask "what" questions.
   — Hear from all parties involved.

4. Restate the problem.
   — Repeat the information you have observed and heard.
5. Ask for children's ideas for solutions, and choose one together.
   — Ask the children for ideas and agreements.
6. Give follow-up support.
   — Tell the children, "You solved the problem!"
   — Check to make sure the solution is acceptable to the children and is carried out as planned.

them resolve conflicts. Adults participate as partners in children's activities rather than as supervisors or managers. They respect children and their choices and encourage initiative, independence, and creativity. Guided by the child development principles outlined in the KDIs and by their observations of children's interests, they provide materials and plan experiences that children need in order to grow and learn. They support children in resolving conflicts by using the six conflict resolution steps outlined on page 8.

What Happens Each Day in a High/Scope Program: Daily Routine

As adults work side by side with children, they participate with them on their terms.

High/Scope programs follow a predictable sequence of events known as the daily routine. This provides a structure within which children can make choices and follow their interests. Following a consistent routine day after day gives children the sense of security they need to be able to make choices and take risks, which will open the door to exciting learning opportunities. Although each High/Scope program decides on the routine that works best for its setting, schedule, and population, the segments described in the following section are always included during the program day. Whatever terminology they use to label parts of the daily routine, adults in the High/Scope program take care to use the names consistently. This allows children to become familiar with the terms and, therefore, able to anticipate the next part of the routine. This, in turn, gives children a sense of security and control over their day.

Components of the High/Scope Daily Routine

Greeting time. This part of the routine usually begins the day in the classroom, whether the day begins in the morning or the afternoon. At greeting time, the teachers, the chil-

dren, and sometimes the parents come together and greet each other informally by talking to each other as they come in. This is a good time to have books available to read with or to the children, so that teachers can encourage parents to read to or with their child to help ease that transition from home to school each day. Also during greeting time teachers use the message board to convey information pertaining to the news of the day in the classroom (e.g., something different happening that is not a normal part of the daily routine, such as a visitor or a field trip). Information on the message board is depicted in pictures, symbols, and words to help enhance children's literacy skills. The message board helps children to know what to expect, and if used consistently every day, children become familiar with letters and words as they are introduced to them with symbols for easier understanding.

Plan-do-review time. This three-part sequence is unique to the High/Scope Curriculum. It includes a 5- to 10-minute period during which children plan what they want to do during work time (the area to visit, materials to use, and friends to play with); a 45- to 60-minute work time for carrying out their plans; and another 5- to 10-minute period for reviewing and recalling with an adult and other children what they've done and learned. In between "do" and "review," children clean up by putting away their materials or storing unfinished projects. Generally, the older the children, the longer and more detailed their planning and review times become.

Work time is the "do" part of the plan-do-review sequence. This 45- to 60-minute period of time for carrying out their plans is an exciting time of freedom and choices for children. Children are very active and purposeful during the "do" portions because they are pursuing activities that interest them. They may follow their initial plans, but often, as they become engaged, their plans shift or may even change completely. Children are not required to follow their original plan but instead are given room to change their plan

based on their interests, new ideas, and discoveries. They have endless opportunities within a safe environment to create and imagine, all the while receiving encouragement, support, and positive feedback from adults. It is during work time where many teachers record most of their daily anecdotes — brief notes describing what children do and say. This process is done as a part of the COR, which is described later in this chapter under How High/Scope Assesses Children.

The plan-do-review sequence can occur at the beginning or end of the day, before or after small-group time or outside time, or once in the morning and once in the afternoon. However, the individual segments of the plan-do-review sequence should always occur in a specific and uninterrupted order: planning should always be immediately followed by work time and cleanup time, which should be followed by recall time. Keeping these segments together enables children to begin making the connection between think-

In this small-group time, the children are painting three-dimensional objects and are showing the teacher (and each other) which objects they chose to paint.

ing about their ideas, putting them into action, and reflecting on those ideas and actions. For more detailed information on High/Scope's plan-do-review, see the Teacher's Idea Book, *Making the Most of Plan-Do-Review* by Nancy Vogel (High/Scope Press, 2001).

Small-group time. During small-group time, children meet with a teacher to experiment with materials, try out new skills, and solve problems. Teachers develop a small-group activity based on children's interests to emphasize one or more particular KDIs while children make choices about how to use the materials and freely communicate their ideas. The length of small group varies with the children's age, interests, and engagement, but usually teachers allow at least 15 minutes in the daily routine for this segment. At the end of the small-group time, children help with cleanup. For more detailed information on High/Scope's small-group times, you may want to look at *Explore and Learn Quick Cards: 80 Activities for Small Groups* by Michelle Graves (High/Scope Press, 2007).

Sample Daily Routines

Half-Day Program
- Greeting time
- Planning, work, cleanup, and recall time
- Snack
- Large-group time
- Small-group time
- Outside time
- Departure

Morning arrival group
- Greeting time
- Planning, work, cleanup, and recall time
- Small-group time
- Large-group time
- Outside time
- Lunch
- Departure

Afternoon arrival group
- Lunch
- Greeting time
- Large-group time
- Planning, work, cleanup, and recall time
- Small-group time
- Snack
- Outside time
- Departure

Full-Day Program
- Breakfast
- Greeting time
- Large-group time
- Planning, work, cleanup, and recall time
- Small-group time
- Outside time
- Lunch
- Books and rest
- Snack
- Outside time
- Departure

Program With Staggered Arrivals and Departures Through the Day
- Free play
- Breakfast
- Greeting time
- Planning, work, cleanup, and recall time
- Small-group time
- Large-group time
- Outside time
- Lunch
- Books and rest
- Snack
- Small-group time
- Planning, work, and cleanup, and recall time with parents

Source: Epstein (2007), p. 57.

Large-group time. Large-group time builds a sense of community. All of the children and all of the adults come together for movement and music activities, interactive storytelling, group and cooperative games, and other shared experiences. Children have many opportunities to make choices and play the role of leader. For more detailed information on High/Scope's large-group times, see *Explore and Learn Quick Cards: 50 Activities for Large Groups* by Christine Boisvert and Suzanne Gainsley (High/Scope Press, 2008) or the Teacher's Idea Book *50 Large-Group Activities for Active Learners* (High/Scope Press, 2006).

Outside time. Children and adults spend at least 30 minutes outside every day, enjoying vigorous and often noisy play in the fresh air. Without the constraints of four walls, they feel freer to make large movements and experiment with the full range of their voices. Children run, climb, swing, roll, jump, yell, and sing with energy. They experience the wonders of nature, including collecting, gardening, and examining wildlife. The adult's role during outside time is to use the same adult-child interaction strategies as during work time: to be involved and engaging with the children. During extreme weather or other unsafe conditions, adults may use an alternative indoor space, if available in their program. Otherwise, they may plan a more active large-group time or extend a work-time segment. For more detailed information on High/Scope's outside times, see *Let's Go Outside! Designing the Early Childhood Playground* by Tracy Theemes (High/Scope Press, 1999).

Transition times. Transitions are the minutes between other blocks of the day, as well as arrival and departure times. Adults strive to make transitions pass smoothly, since they set the stage for the next segment in the day's schedule. They also provide meaningful learning opportunities themselves, especially in the area of litera-

cy, language, and math. Whenever possible, High/Scope teachers give children choices about how to make a transition. For example, children may choose how to move across the floor on their way to small-group time or other parts of the daily routine. With consistent daily routines children know what is going to take place next, and it is not unusual for children to announce the next activity and initiate the transition. For more information on transitions and how to make them meaningful, see the Teacher's Idea Book, *"I Know What's Next!" Preschool Transitions Without Tears or Turmoil* by Betsy Evans (High/Scope Press, 2007).

Eating and resting times. Meals and snacks allow children to enjoy eating healthy food in a supportive social setting. Rest is for quiet, solitary activities. Since both activities happen at home as well as at school, adults in High/Scope programs try to respect family customs at these times as much as possible. A primary goal is to create a shared and secure sense of community within the program.

Considerations for Setting Up the Daily Routine

Every program organizes its daily routine, including the plan-do-review sequence, to meet the needs of the children and families it serves. As adults think about how to schedule plan-do-review for a Head Start program, they take a number of program factors into consideration as well. If the children arrive at different times throughout the morning of a full-day classroom, it might make sense for adults to schedule planning, work, and recall time after most or all children have arrived, rather than first thing in the morning, when only a handful of children are present. On the other hand, if children all arrive at the same time, the plan-do-review sequence could begin right away.

Adults may also need to work around the local conditions that influence an outdoor play space or multipurpose room. When arranging the program routine, consider the amount of time available, children's arrival and departure times, licensing requirements (such as rest time), and any specific times activities must occur in a certain place (for meals, outdoor play, special events, and so on). It is then possible to work the High/Scope daily routine components into the schedule, keeping in mind the recommended times for each segment and keeping the plan-do-review sequence together. (See p. 18 for a list of daily routine components.)

Adults in a High/Scope program organize the parts of the day in a logical fashion, just as they do their own personal routine, so the day flows smoothly. They avoid building in unnecessary transitions, such as having children remove all their outdoor wear after playing outside and then putting it back on again to go home after a brief indoor large-group time.

What a High/Scope Setting Looks Like: Learning Environment

The space and materials in a High/Scope setting are carefully chosen and arranged to promote active participatory learning. Although the High/Scope Foundation does not endorse specific types or brands of toys and equipment, it does provide general guidelines and recommendations for selecting materials that are meaningful and interesting to children. The learning environment in High/Scope programs

▼ Is welcoming to children

▼ Provides enough materials for all the children

▼ Is organized and labeled to allow children to find, use, and return materials independently

▼ Encourages different types of play

▼ Allows the children to see and easily

move through all the areas of the classroom or center

▼ Is flexible so children can extend their play by bringing materials from one area to another

▼ Offers a variety of open-ended materials, including materials that reflect the diversity of children's family lives

Room Arrangement

The High/Scope Curriculum emphasizes careful attention to **arranging and equipping the classroom or center** in order to provide an environment that is stimulating but ordered — one in which children can make choices and act upon those choices. The environment is designed to encourage both social interaction and solitary play, and to provide comfortable spaces for both individual and group activities. To encourage children's self-reliance and purposeful play, the space is divided into **interest areas:** for example, house, art, block, book and toy areas, using simple terms that children will understand, instead of manipulative or dramatic play area. Each area is stocked with a rich variety of materials (real, toy, and natural) and tools; these materials are well organized, clearly labeled, and accessible to children. Children know where materials are,

In a High/Scope classroom, the room is clearly divided into interest areas. Each interest area is stocked with materials that children can easily find, use, and put away.

and they can get them out and put them away without adult help.

Working and Planning as a Team

Adults in programs based on the High/Scope Curriculum use a **team approach.** For teams to be effective, all team members spend a portion of each day meeting together to review the previous day's activities and to plan for the next day. This is called *daily team planning,* and this brings together the experiences, interests, and strengths of each adult. In parallel with its approach of supporting the development of young children, High/Scope furthers the belief that, in the context of supportive team membership, each adult's unique capabilities will flourish. The following are just some of the benefits of team planning:

▼ Increased support and training for individual staff members

▼ An opportunity for team members to learn from one another

▼ A forum for idea exchange and debate

▼ A cooperative approach to problem solving

How High/Scope Assesses Children

High/Scope assesses children's development with comprehensive observations using the Preschool Child Observation Record (COR) and the Child Observation Record (COR) for Infants and Toddlers, both of which are research based, valid, and reliable instruments. Observing a broad range of behaviors over several weeks or months provides an in-depth picture of children's true capabilities. Using the KDIs as a framework, teachers record daily "anecdotes" — brief notes describing what children do and say. Two or three times a year, they review these anecdotes and rate each child at the highest level he or she has demonstrated so far on 32

items in six areas of development (initiative, social relations, creative representation, movement and music, language and literacy, and mathematics and science), which coordinate with the KDIs. Children's COR scores help teachers design learning opportunities tailored to their level of development.

The COR is used to explain children's progress to parents during conferences. Instead of only giving parents abstract scores, teachers share anecdotes illustrating what their children are doing now and how they will continue to grow. High/Scope has also used the COR in state and national research projects to investigate the effectiveness of its educational approach and to compare it to other curriculum models.

The anecdotal notes that teachers write each day are certainly a vital part of the assessment of children; they are also a vital part for planning activities that will support the children where they are developmentally. There is a misconception that anecdote note taking is to be done separately, in which teachers sit on the sidelines, simply observe the children, and write down their observations in an anecdote note form. For anecdotes to be most meaningful, teachers should be jotting down notes *while* they are interacting with the children during the daily rou-

Work time is an ideal time to quickly jot down anecdotal notes; this teacher uses a clipboard that she can bring with her while she is interacting with the children.

tine and especially during work time. Work time is when High/Scope teachers use the adult-child interaction strategies with children to help support the plans that the children have made during planning time. The anecdotes should be briefly written at the same time while the teachers are involved in the children's play and are extending on children's plans and ideas. In fact, the teacher's involvement will, more than likely, enhance the notes he or she takes on the children. The teacher's engagement can often extend the child's plans and learning, which will make for more accurate notes on the child's abilities and interests.

How High/Scope Evaluates Programs

A proven model can only benefit children if it is implemented with high levels of fidelity. To guarantee that programs claiming to do High/Scope are indeed using the High/Scope educational approach, the High/Scope Foundation certifies teachers and trainers, and accredits programs with the Preschool Program Quality Assessment (PQA). Trained evaluators observe in the classroom and interview program staff to record objective notes and complete ratings on 63 items in seven areas: learning environment, daily routine, adult-child interaction, curriculum planning and assessment, parent involvement and family services, staff qualifications and staff development, and program management. The PQA also serves as a useful tool for staff development, because detailed examples of "ideal" implementation are built into the scoring system. Like the COR, the PQA is also used in state and national evaluation projects to assess the impact of training and to examine the relationship between program quality and children's development. Finally, of special relevance to Head Start programs, the PQA has been aligned with the HSPPS

(High/Scope, 2003b), and Head Start programs can use the PQA to prepare for site visits, such as for peer reviews from the Office of Regional Operations.

High/Scope Accountability Standards

High/Scope KDIs and assessment tools can be aligned with the teaching standards and child outcomes required by states, school districts, and federally funded programs. For example, the High/Scope COR is aligned with specific indicators in the Head Start Child Outcomes Framework, and COR can report COR findings in terms of Head Start Child Outcomes (see Appendix D). Similarly, the Head Start User Guide to the PQA[1] connects each PQA item to the relevant criteria in the HSPPS. The High/Scope Curriculum can also be cross-mapped with the early childhood standards of virtually every local school district or state department of education. As a whole, the High/Scope Curriculum and teaching approach are compatible with the best developmental practices recommended by respected practitioner groups. In developing specific content areas, High/Scope also takes into account the standards and guidelines of relevant professional organizations such as the International Reading Association and the National Council of Teachers of Mathematics.

The High/Scope Demonstration Preschool, in Ypsilanti, Michigan, is accredited by the National Association for the Education of Young Children (NAEYC). (For additional information on NAEYC or NAEYC accreditation, visit the NAEYC Web site.) The Demonstration Preschool is a blended program — it is tuition based and also participates in the Michigan School Readiness Program (MSRP). The MSRP provides funds for preschool programs for four-year-old children who may be at risk of

---

[1]The Head Start User Guide to the PQA is included in the Administration Manual of the Preschool Program Quality Assessment (PQA) Starter Pak, Second Edition. It is also included in Appendix D of this book.

school failure (see the MSRP Web site for additional information).

High/Scope Training

High/Scope trains administrators, curriculum specialists, teachers, and child care providers in the High/Scope approach. Training also prepares participants to work directly with parents. The training sessions are held at individual program locations and at Foundation headquarters in Ypsilanti, Michigan, where the High/Scope Demonstration Preschool is visited by hundreds of educators each year. In the past 30 years, High/Scope has conducted training in every state and in more than 20 foreign countries. The Foundation also holds an annual international conference on education in Michigan as well as several regional conferences throughout the year.

To accommodate different training needs and schedules, High/Scope offers a variety of courses and workshops ranging from one day to multiple weeks spread over several months. High/Scope also offers online training courses, in which participants join an e-learning community and have access to group discussions as well as individual attention from the course instructor.

Training combines theory with practical application. The High/Scope Curriculum courses cover all aspects of understanding and implementing the educational approach with children and youth. Adult training courses enable those in supervisory positions to train and support staff at their own agencies as they use the High/Scope model. In addition to these basic courses, High/Scope also offers an ever-expanding roster of advanced workshops and seminars on such topics as reading, assessment, conflict resolution, visual and performing arts, and staff supervision.

High/Scope has collaborative arrangements with institutions of higher education, enabling participants to earn undergraduate or graduate credit for attending training. Successful completion of High/Scope course work also results in teacher or trainer certification, or program accreditation, based on rigorous evaluation criteria including assessment with the PQA. Individuals and agencies who are certified or accredited, respectively, become members of the High/Scope International Registry. Anyone with an interest in High/Scope can also join the High/Scope Membership Association to receive updated information about Foundation activities as well as free periodicals and discounts on Foundation conferences and products.

Additional information about High/Scope training and materials is available at High/Scope's Web site (*www.highscope.org*).

Meeting the Challenge

Now that you have an overview of what High/Scope is all about, you can get a "head start" on implementing High/Scope in your program by learning about the issues that others working in Head Start programs often face. You can begin by reading the remainder of this book while thinking about the unique features and needs of your own program and the children it serves.

2

Special Issues in Head Start Preschool Programs

You may be implementing a Head Start program in any one of a variety of early childhood program types: those serving preschool children, infants/toddlers (Early Head Start), children with special needs, children from linguistically diverse backgrounds, children at risk of school failure, or children from families of migrants or seasonal workers (Migrant Head Start). Your program may be located at an early childhood education center, a campus-based center, a corporate center, a child care collaboration center, in a public school, in a home-based center, or maybe even in a church basement. All Head Start programs, however, have one thing in common: serving a diverse group of economically disadvantaged children and their families. Although there are differences from state to state in terms of requirements for adult-child ratios, teacher education, licensing requirements, and other details, all Head Start programs are governed by the same federally funded mandates and guidelines, the Head Start Program Performance Standards (HSPPS).

Head Start programs, in addition to providing the nurturing care required of any early childhood program, must also meet their mandate to promote young children's school readiness, defined broadly to encompass social and cognitive development. Compared to the rest of the population, Head Start children and their families, by definition, have lower household incomes. Head Start programs also serve a high percentage of children with disabilities and other special needs (12 percent) as well as members of minority groups (60 percent) and English language learners (almost 28 percent of Head Start children are from families where English is not the primary language) (Head Start English Language Learners Project, n.d.; U. S. Department of Health and Human Services [DHHS], 2007a). The individual and family stresses that result from these conditions place special demands on Head Start programs to provide effective and comprehensive service to the children and families they serve. Teachers and administrators in Head Start programs can meet these needs of young children and their families by also meeting the challenges and issues that arise while implementing the High/Scope Curriculum, which include

▼ Planning a flexible daily routine

▼ Connecting Head Start content areas and Child Outcomes with the High/Scope Curriculum

▼ Conducting effective small-group times

▼ Including families in the program

▼ Collaborating effectively with other adults

This chapter addresses these issues so that you can meet the needs of the children and families you serve.

Planning a Flexible Daily Routine

Children develop a sense of security when they are able to predict events within their day. As children participate in a consistent and flexible daily routine, they are able to relax and feel secure in knowing what to expect. Additionally, the stability of a daily routine helps the classroom adults plan activities that meet the needs of every child. The elements of the High/Scope daily routine include

▼ Greeting time (variable)

▼ Planning time (5–10 minutes)

▼ Work time (45–60 minutes)

▼ Cleanup time (10 minutes)

▼ Recall time (5–10 minutes)

▼ Small-group time (15–20 minutes)

▼ Large-group time (15–20 minutes)

▼ Outside time (30–40 minutes)

For Head Start classrooms, you will need to add

▼ Mealtimes (breakfast, lunch, and/or snack, depending on the time and length of the program day)

▼ Tooth brushing

▼ Naptime (if a full-day program)

These elements may be used in any order, with the exception that the planning time, work time, cleanup time, and recall time (also called **plan-do-review**) follow each other and always stay in that order. This is the key to why High/Scope's daily routine can be used successfully in completely different types of programs — teachers are able to piece together the components of the daily routine in the most meaningful way for their individual classrooms. For example, classrooms in your particular Head Start center might have completely different routines because of the need to schedule around playground availability; bathroom availability; supplemental services providers, such as special needs assistants, bilingual consultants, speech therapists, and so forth; or other considerations. Furthermore, your half-day program may have a different daily routine in the morning than your program in the afternoon. When you begin planning your routine based on your children's needs, you will see that children are different and respond differently during different parts of the day. Once your program or classroom has decided on a routine, however, it is important to keep it as predictable and consistent as possible each day so the children develop a sense of security in knowing what to expect.

Depending on the needs of a specific community, times and settings vary for Head Start programs. When Head Start first began in 1965, it was a half-day summer program. Today programs operate throughout the school year (some for the full year), and many offer full-day classrooms or collaborate with local child care programs for wraparound services. These full-day (and sometimes full-year) programs evolved in most states because of the Personal Responsibility and Work Opportunity Reconciliation Act of 1996, popularly known as the welfare reform bill. Because of this law, more Head Start parents who used to be stay-at-home parents are in the workforce and need all-day care for their children.

To meet the physical as well as cognitive, emotional, and social needs of young children in a full-day active participatory learning environment, it is critical to recognize the need for flexibility and variation throughout a long day. Although children have a lot of energy, scheduled "downtime" is necessary as well as opportunities for children to be alone, rather than in a group. The High/Scope daily routine can help you find balance among such issues while accommodating personal care routines such as naptime and mealtime.

The two aspects of the daily routine most salient to their implementation in a Head Start program are the nutrition and health components. Child nutrition is one of the main components of the Head Start program. Because of this, mealtimes, tooth brushing, and naptime play an important part in Head Start classrooms.

Nutrition

Whether you offer a full- or a half-day program, mealtimes must be part of your daily routine. The HSPPS clearly state that Head Start programs must design and implement a nutrition program that meets the nutritional needs of each individual child enrolled, including those with special dietary needs. It further states that each child in a center-based setting must receive at least one third of the child's daily nutritional needs if in a half-day program and at least one half to two thirds of the child's nutritional needs if in a full-day program. The nutrition program your Head Start center implements should offer children a variety of food, which will broaden their food experiences, and give children opportunities to participate in food-related activities. Family-style serving is also part of this mandate, which means that all children and all assigned classroom staff, including volunteers, eat together and share

the same menu, in which the food is placed on the table and children serve themselves (HSPPS, 2006). Primary funding for the meals served must come from a USDA Food and Nutrition Service Child Nutrition Program (HSPPS 1304.23, 2006).

Learning often naturally occurs at mealtimes. This child is matching straws with milk containers, which helps develop her mathematic skills.

Most Head Start programs use the Child and Adult Care Food Program (CACFP) to satisfy this mandate. The CACFP comes with its own set of guidelines and regulations that Head Start programs must adhere to, including the regulation of "point of service," when adults must take attendance at the time the children are served their meals so that the Head Start program receives funds for that meal. Many adults in Head Start programs using the High/Scope Curriculum feel this is a tedious task. However, it does not have to be done with all of the fanfare of announcing children's names and having them respond in a roll-call fashion. Many adults feel this takes away from that shared and secure sense of

Key Developmental Indicators at Mealtimes

Mealtimes are a wonderful opportunity for children to interact with each other and adults in a relaxed setting; it is also an opportunity for teachers to observe key developmental indicators. Below is a list of commonly heard remarks from children about food; note how they might be used by teachers as anecdotal observations. Remember, learning experiences happen naturally all day long, so don't overlook what happens during mealtimes!

Language, Literacy, and Communication

Talking with others about personally meaningful experiences

Any genuine conversation between children and adults allows children time to share things that are important to them. This is one reason why meals in Head Start programs and in programs following the High/Scope Curriculum are served "family style" — so that children and adults can learn more about each other!

Social and Emotional Development

Taking care of one's own needs

After a child spills a drink, she gets up and runs for a paper towel.

Child asks for the sandwiches to be passed so he can take another one.

Mathematics: Seriation

Comparing attributes (longer/shorter, bigger/smaller)

Child — "This carrot is BIG. I got the biggest one!"

Mathematics: Number

Counting objects

Child — "I don't like those. I only want one."

Mathematics: Space

Changing the shape and arrangement of objects (wrapping, twisting, stretching, stacking, enclosing)

Child hides a piece of broccoli in a napkin.

Science and Technology: Classification

Distinguishing and describing shapes

Child — "Hey this bread is a square!"

Science and Technology: Time

Starting and stopping an action on signal

Child pours milk from a pitcher to a cup.

Social Studies

Participating in group routines

After finishing the food, child takes her plate and puts it in the garbage and then goes to the couch to read a book.

The Arts: Visual Art

Relating models, pictures, and photographs to real places and things

Child — "Look! This cracker looks like a sun!"

community within the classroom they are trying to create during mealtimes, especially when they take attendance in a more playful way at greeting time. According to the CACFP guidelines, point of service must be taken at all mealtimes by checking off or marking with an *X* if a child is present (or not) on a consistent form provided by the CACFP. However, no where do the CACFP guidelines state that it has to be done verbally. Thus, adults in Head Start programs can adhere to these guidelines while incorporating their own way of taking attendance at greeting time.

Dental Health

Along with the nutrition component is dental health. According to the HSPPS 1304.23(b)(3), Head Start staff must pro-

mote effective dental hygiene among children in conjunction with meals by assisting children ages two and over in brushing their teeth using a small smear of fluoride toothpaste (HSPPS, 2006). Clearly, tooth brushing needs to be part of every Head Start program's daily routine.

Many Head Start teachers using the High/Scope Curriculum have found it challenging to include tooth brushing in the daily routine. Some try to include it in work time by having the children stop their plans to come and brush teeth; however, this is not an ideal way to incorporate this component. First, work time, the "do" of plan-do-review, is the only time when children carry out their plans that they made during planning time. If we ask them to stop and come

Incorporating tooth brushing with children's bathroom time right after a designated meal is one way to meet the challenge of tooth brushing in the daily routine — keeping the area organized and well stocked with appropriate supplies helps as well.

to an activity that we, as adults, planned (even if it is for their own good health), then why are we asking children to make plans if they will not be able to carry them out without interruption? Second, tooth brushing during work time is considered low quality according to High/Scope's Preschool Program Quality Assessment (PQA) (PQA item II-E; see High/Scope Educational Research Foundation, 2003b). If you are striving to provide a high-quality program in your Head Start program, you will want to find other ways to meet the challenge of tooth brushing in the daily routine. Here are some suggestions:

▼ **Incorporate the tooth brushing with children's bathroom time right after a designated meal.** You don't have to wait for everyone to finish their meal before children begin tooth brushing. Solicit extra adult help during this time if you do not have a sink in the classroom or access to a nearby bathroom. The extra adult help can be a parent volunteer (which will help you incorporate your parent involvement component) or a nonteaching staff member such as a family service worker or a cook (tooth brushing *is* part of the cook's component).

▼ **Make sure you are not adding undue stress by cramming too much in your daily routine.** Remember, the HSPPS only require you to have children brush teeth once a day, after one meal. As you consider your children's needs, temperaments, and your daily routine, decide with your coteachers which meal that would be. For a half-day program, you have a choice of after breakfast or after lunch. In a full-day program, you have a choice of three meals: after breakfast, lunch, or snack. Remember that the importance of the activity is to help promote and instill good dental hygiene in the children, so it is important to think about the learning that can happen at tooth-brushing time as well as the lasting effects on the children's oral health.

Physical Activity

Current literature on the increase in childhood obesity, of particular concern in economically disadvantaged populations such as those served by Head Start, emphasizes that daily physical activity, along with a healthy diet, is important in preventing and reversing the health risks associated with being overweight. Head Start acknowledges that physical health is an important component of development, and the High/Scope Curriculum supports this recognition in its emphasis on outdoor play. Because outside time offers so many educational options, it supports many areas of the Head Start mandate for young children's development.

Outside time in High/Scope programs is an active participatory learning time of equal importance to the active participatory learning that takes place indoors. Just as adults partner with children during indoor play, they are also active participants in young children's outdoor play. In other words, outside time is not when adults stand around and talk to one another while keeping an eye on children's safety. Outside time in High/Scope programs is a period of active physical engagement for everyone! Even children whose mobility is limited by physical disabilities can enjoy the fresh air, the opportunity to exercise mobile limbs or to be moved from place to place with their peers, and to explore the outdoor environment.

Outside time happens every day in High/Scope programs and lasts at least 30 minutes. Children and adults enjoy vigorous and often noisy play in the fresh air while running, climbing, swinging, rolling, jumping, and yelling with energy. There are many opportunities for physical activity, social interaction, language development, and learning about nature and the environment. While children enjoy using large outdoor equipment (such as wheeled toys and slides), even programs with limited budgets can provide

The adults in this program use the daily walk to the city playground as an opportunity for the children to practice traffic safety.

appropriate outside times by recognizing that children's bodies can be "equipment" enough for learning.

In addition, the High/Scope standards for creating a safe outdoor environment are compatible with the health and safety requirements for Head Start programs. They take into account such factors as the average amount of space per child and procedures for guaranteeing that outdoor equipment is well maintained. For specific requirements, see Appendix D for the alignment of the HSPPS and the PQA.

Some Head Start programs may have difficulty implementing the "outside" part of this High/Scope curriculum component because of their location and/or weather conditions. For example, not all sites have easy access to an adjoining playground. In such cases, there may be a nearby play area,

such as a city park or school playground and athletic field, or a church where outside time can occur. (Most such facilities will make arrangements for Head Start programs to use their outdoor areas.)

Some urban programs have even been known to create safe playgrounds on the rooftop, often with active and enthusiastic help from parents. If no outdoor area is nearby, or considered safe for the neighborhood where the program is located, a large gym can be used to provide an open space for vigorous physical activity. However, a gym is not a perfect alternative to going outside and should only be the choice of **last** resort — there is a certain transformation that occurs when children are playing outdoors that can not be replicated indoors. In climates or at times of the year where the weather is too extreme for children to be outdoors, an

During outside time, children exercise their large muscles and explore a new environment.

Tips for Repeating Parts of the Daily Routine

- When repeating work time during the program day, build in additional planning and recalling to allow children to extend their planning and recalling skills and work-time activities.

- Employ adult-child work-time interaction strategies that encourage and stimulate children's play.

- Rotate toys and introduce items in play areas that help build on children's play and keep them engaged.

- Use strategies for group times, work time, and planning and recalling that reflect the energy level of the children. Use quiet strategies when children are tired, and use more noisy, physical strategies when children's energy is high.

- Vary group activities; use staff members who arrive in the afternoon for activity ideas that reflect the children's interests and energy levels.

expansive indoor area will also suffice. However, remember that as long as children are adequately dressed, they can play outdoors for brief periods of time with no risk to health and safety. Don't let your own reluctance to go outside limit the options you offer children.

Full-Day Programs

Full-day Head Start programs have enough time in the day to implement each piece of the High/Scope daily routine and usually more. Depending on the amount of time your program has available in the afternoon, you may plan to repeat the entire

plan-do-review process in addition to another group time. In some cases, you might need to shorten the afternoon work-time segment, but the plan-do-review sequence will remain the same. If each part of the daily routine is planned around the recommended durations — such as 45–60 minutes for work time — then, with a period for outside time, most of the morning is scheduled up to lunchtime. After lunch, the children will have a rest period and then awake to snack. The afternoons tend to be more relaxed and low key, but it is still necessary to have a routine.

For more information on implementing a full-day High/Scope program, see *Building a High/Scope Program: Full-Day Preschool Programs* by Tricia S. Kruse (High/Scope Press, 2005).

Connecting Head Start Content Areas and Child Outcomes With the High/Scope Curriculum

Head Start Content Areas

Head Start works because it is concerned with the whole child, which is why there are so many content areas involved in its program. These content areas are directly from the HSPPS; each one has its own section to explain how it is carried out in the program. The nine content areas in Head Start include:

1. Education
2. Nutrition
3. Health and safety
4. Mental health
5. Disability services
6. Social services
7. Family literacy
8. Parent involvement
9. Family and community partnerships

Head Start content area specialists or coordinators, part of Head Start's administrative team, are knowledgeable in their specific content area and can assist a center's or program's staff in carrying out the mandates that pertain to their content areas. Head Start teachers are required to incorporate these content areas in their classrooms and in their lesson plans. To some, this may seem like an overwhelming task, but adults in Head Start programs who use High/Scope will find that the High/Scope Curriculum addresses the same, or comparable, content areas. (For more information, see Epstein [2007], Part 3.)

As you plan your day with your children in mind, you can see where the content areas can fit in with the daily routine. Much of this has to do with your learning environment — making sure you have open-ended

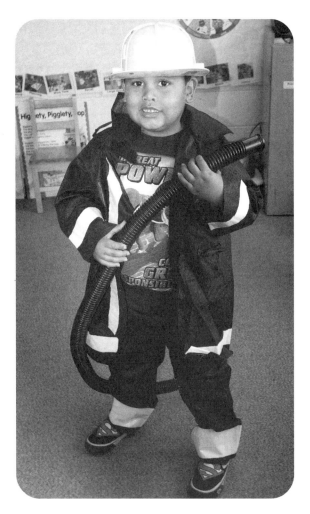

Stocking the house area with different dress-up clothing is one way Head Start teachers can incorporate a content area in their daily routine.

materials that lend themselves to some of the content areas in your classroom is half the battle. For example, if you want to promote health and safety (one of the Head Start content areas) in your classroom, make sure you have in your house area dress-up clothes that reflect firefighter outfits; doctor kits; and, perhaps, a crossing guard vest. You can use life jackets, floats, and other materials to introduce safety concepts and add miniature traffic signs with small vehicles to the block area to introduce traffic safety. Once you've added materials, you can see how the children use them during work time and then plan activities based on their use and interests that will further promote this content

Head Start's Legislatively Mandated
Language Development and Literacy Indicators

Domain	Domain Element	Indicators
Language Development	Listening & Understanding	★ Understands an increasingly complex and varied vocabulary. ★ For non-English-speaking children, progresses in listening to and understanding English.
	Speaking & Communicating	★ Develops increasing abilities to understand and use language to communicate information, experiences, ideas, feelings, opinions, needs, questions; and for other varied purposes. ★ Uses an increasingly complex and varied spoken vocabulary. ★ For non-English-speaking children, progresses in speaking English.
Literacy	Phonological Awareness	★ Associates sounds with written words, such as awareness that different words begin with the same sound.
	Print Awareness & Concepts	★ Recognizes a word as a unit of print, or awareness that letters are grouped to form words, and that words are separated by spaces.
	Alphabet Knowledge	★ Identifies at least 10 letters of the alphabet, especially those in their own name. ★ Knows that letters of the alphabet are a special category of visual graphics that can be individually named.

★ *Indicates the Indicators that are legislatively mandated.*

Source: U.S. Department of Health and Human Services (2003).

area. The activities that you plan can be used for a brief planning or recall strategy, a small-group-time activity, or a large-group activity. This same technique can be used with all of the content areas. This will make it a little easier for the adults and, more important, more meaningful to the children. Don't forget that you have a content area

specialist or a coordinator that you can also use as a resource for ideas of incorporating the content areas in your daily routine.

Head Start Domains

The Head Start Child Outcomes Framework is intended to guide Head Start programs in their ongoing assessment of the progress and accomplishments of 3–5-year-old children and in efforts to analyze and use data on child outcomes in program self-assessments and continuous improvement. It is based on the HSPPS, performance measures, and provision of Head Start as amended in 1998. The Outcomes Framework was developed independently from the HSPPS (which were specifically intended for programs, not children) to guide the progress and accomplishments of children. The Outcomes Framework and mandated Domain Elements and Indicators were created in 2000; the Domains, Domain Elements, and Indicators are presented as building blocks that are important for school success.

The framework is composed of 8 Domains; 27 Domain Elements; and 100 examples of more specific Indicators of children's skills, abilities, knowledge, and behaviors. Four specific Domain Elements and nine Indicators from the Domain Elements (under Language Development and Literacy) are legislatively mandated (see the chart on p. 26 for the legislatively mandated Indicators).

For a complete list of the Domains, Domain Elements, and Indicators, see Appendix C.

Language and Literacy

In 2002, the federal government launched Good Start, Grow Smart, an early childhood initiative to strengthen Head Start; partner with states to improve early childhood education; and provide information to teachers, caregivers, and parents. In response to this initiative, the Head Start Bureau developed Project STEP, Head Start's Summer Teacher Education Program, to provide training to teachers in early literacy teaching techniques that would help children's progress in early language and prereading skills (DHHS, 2002). Because of Head Start's emphasis on language and literacy, many programs have adopted a curriculum to specifically address these important areas of development. Toward that end,

High/Scope has developed and validated the Growing Readers Early Literacy Curriculum (High/Scope, 2005).

The Growing Readers Early Literacy Curriculum (GRC) is a set of detailed plans for teacher-led, small-group activities that engage young children in four areas comparable to the Head Start Domain Elements: comprehension (including listening and understanding as well as speaking and communicating), phono-

Sharing a book with children is a great way to initiate natural and interesting conversations with them.

logical awareness, alphabetic principle, and concepts about print. The curriculum recommends children's books that can be used in the activities; sets of books with characters and stories from diverse backgrounds and cultures can be purchased through High/Scope.

In addition, High/Scope has developed an authentic assessment tool in the form of a storybook, the Early Literacy Skills Assessment (ELSA) (High/Scope, 2004) to monitor children's progress in these literacy domains and plan effectively for individual children and the class as a whole. The characters in the storybook are animals, so the story appeals to children of all backgrounds. An assessor, usually the child's teacher, reads the storybook and asks the child questions that are meaningful in the context of the story.

The ELSA meets scientific standards of reliability and validity (DeBruin-Parecki, 2004). The storybook is available in two versions (one for the first year of assessment; the second version can be used for the second year of assessment, if necessary) and in English and Spanish: *Violet's Adventure (La Aventura de Violeta)* and *Dante Grows Up (El Cambio en Dante)*.

Many Head Start programs are using the GRC to meet the Head Start Domain Element of Literacy and administering the ELSA to document children's progress. The GRC was validated in a diverse national sample of 82 teachers and 630 preschool children, comprising children from Head Start, English language learners, and children with special needs. Children in classrooms using the GRC made significant pre- to post-treatment gains on the ELSA in all four areas of literacy knowledge and skills (High/Scope, 2005). For more information on the GRC

and ELSA, visit the Early Literacy section at High/Scope's Web site (*www.highscope.org*).

Even before the national emphasis on early literacy in Head Start and the development of specialized program materials and assessment tools (High/Scope's GRC and ELSA), the High/Scope Curriculum has always emphasized language and literacy development and offered many practical strategies for promoting this domain in young children. To support language development, the most important factor is to talk to children in your program. The more young children are exposed to language, especially a rich and varied vocabulary, the better their later literacy skills (Hart & Risley, 1995).

To support early reading skills, your classroom should be a print-rich learning environment with materials and areas effectively labeled; that is, having a variety of labels throughout your classroom that exposes children to print pictures and words. The

The Message Board

Not only does the message board provide learning opportunities for time concepts such as *first, second,* and *third* and *yesterday, today,* and *tomorrow,* it also is an activity rich in literacy experiences. Children become familiar with letters and words as they are introduced to them each day when combined with simple symbols for easier understanding. Many teachers have found that by placing a message board in a place accessible to children, the children will frequently make writing attempts throughout the day. Another possibility is to write the messages on 8½ by 11-inch paper and post them next to one another as the week progresses. Then, at the end of the week, you can make a book out of them by stapling them together or punching holes in each piece of paper and tying them together with string. The teacher could review the week with the children on the following Monday, and then leave the book out in the book area for the children to revisit. For more informa-

tion, see *From Message to Meaning: Using a Daily Message Board in the Preschool Classroom* by Suzanne Gainsley (High/Scope Press, 2008).

interest areas or learning centers in your classroom should all have simple names that make sense to children; these names should be indicated with words, pictures, or objects. The classroom equipment and materials should also be named with different labels, including drawings, photocopies, catalog pictures, words, or photographs. This system allows children at various stages of literacy development to comprehend the labels and practice literacy skills every day.

Here is a list of other things you can do throughout the High/Scope's daily routine to support language and literacy development:

Greeting Time

▼ Have books and writing materials available when children arrive to greeting time and encourage children to read to and engage with each other and talk about the books.

▼ Use the message board (a dry-erase board, easel pad, chalkboard, or similar surface) to communicate through pictures, words, and spoken communication and for alphabet knowledge and sounds by playing guessing games with the first letter in children's names (the first letter of a child's name is usually the first letter that a child learns). For example, have the children guess which child will choose to pick a song from the song book to sing at large-group time by writing on the message board:

I _ _ _ _ _

The children can then guess what letters are missing to fill in the child's name on the message board.

▼ Have children sign in every day just as their parents sign them in for class so

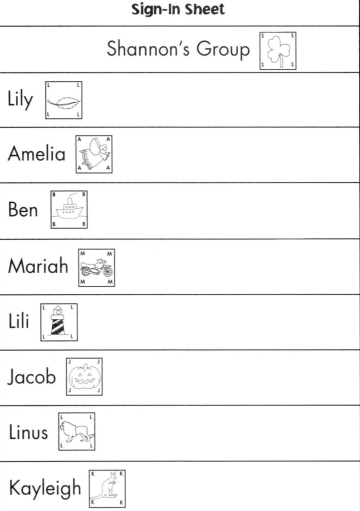

that they can practice their name-writing skills daily. Teachers can use these sign-in sheets (see Shannon's Group sign-in sheet for an example) to show progress in children's writing skills.

Large-Group Time

▼ Plan activities that

– Encourage children to talk about their movements after movement and music activities.

– Give children opportunities to make up songs, fingerplays, and stories (and then write them down).

– Allow children to recite and act out nursery rhymes, encouraging them to portray characters as they recite them as a group. Some favorite rhymes in the Demonstration Preschool include "Rub-a-Dub-Dub," "Jack Be Nimble," "Humpty Dumpty," and "Little Miss Muffet."

Small-Group Time

▼ Use storybooks in your book area to read to your small group and do an activity that coincides with the story.

▼ Plan some small-group times that use alphabet stickers, alphabet cereal, and alphabet letters in different formats to create an alphabet collage.

▼ Provide opportunities for children to dictate or write a group story based on some common element that they have all experienced.

▼ Encourage children to talk about their small-group-time activities by talking to them individually about how they are using the materials.

Planning and Recall Times

▼ Use the letters in children's names to use as a turn-taking strategy for planning or recalling. For example, have the letters of the children's names in a small bag or basket. Pull out a letter; the children's names that begin with that letter knows it is their turn to plan or recall.

▼ Use a planning and recall journal from time to time to encourage children to write down their plans and recalls. To support children with these journals, always have index cards available in your classroom with all the interest areas and their symbols for children to copy. Use index cards as a reference for children's names as well, for when they want to write their or their classmates' names.

▼ Encourage children to talk about their plans and their work-time experiences in a variety of ways (e.g., whisper, sing, use an animal voice or a monster voice).

Mealtimes

▼ Have children sign up for jobs by writing their names next to the desired job (e.g., setting the table).

▼ During snacktimes, allow children to make certain food items. Have them participate in measuring, mixing, and cooking the items. Make a recipe poster and have it where all can see it, or make individual recipe cards for each child.

▼ Discuss nutritional ideas (e.g., milk makes our bones grow strong; vegetables supply vitamins so we have the energy to play). Converse with children about topics they are particularly interested in, making sure that the conversational ideas are tied to concepts young children will understand.

Naptime

▼ Right before naptime, read *The Napping House* by Audrey Wood, and then ask the children to show how they like to fall asleep on their cots.

▼ Have a small basket of books for children to keep near their cots for the ones who don't fall off to sleep right away to look at and read quietly while they are lying on their cots.

▼ Allow children to develop their own list of possible quiet activities that are okay to do if they don't want to sleep. Have them dictate it to you as you write it down, and post it where they nap.

Transition Times

▼ Have the children listen for the first letter of their names to know when to go to the next part of the daily routine. For

Reading a book with a small group of children in a comfortable setting creates a pleasurable reading experience for both adult and child.

example, you might say, "If your name begins with the /B/ sound, go to the coat rack to get ready for outside time. Yes, Brian and Becky are getting their coats." You can also sing the alphabet song slowly, asking the children to leave when their corresponding letter is sung. Alternatively, you can sing an alliterative song, such as "Willaby, Wallaby, Woo," and, together with the children, substitute the initial letter of children's names at the beginning of each word (e.g., "Millaby, Mallaby, Moo") as they transition to the next activity.

▼ Ask the children to listen for the same sound as their name to transition to the next activity. Say, for example, "If your name starts the same as *house*, go to your

planning table." Henry says, "That's me," and goes to his table.

▼ Encourage children to make up a song or tell a story about what they did today while waiting for an activity to start.

Sign Language

Another way to support language and literacy development is by using sign language in your Head Start classroom. Using American Sign Language for the Deaf helps to increase children's vocabulary in a relatively pressure-free manner. Research studies show hearing children who used sign language in their preschool and kindergarten classes scored better on vocabulary tests and attained higher reading levels than their nonsigning peers (Daniels, 2000).

Looking at her friend Evan's letter link and signing the letter E helps this child focus on the individual letter.

Sign language uses a series of hand shapes called the *manual alphabet;* signing the alphabet to make words is called *fingerspelling.* The manual alphabet provides an easy, convenient form of spelling for young children. Children can fingerspell much sooner than they acquire the manual dexterity to write words with pencil and paper. Because young children learn through active, physical experiences, sign language, which can be described as "language in motion," provides a more natural mode for children's language and alphabet acquisition and development than a written language, be it English or a child's native language. The importance of movement to the learning process is exemplified when we as adults anchor a thought with movement by writing it down. Sign language gives children a medium through which they use the movement of the sign itself, as they produce it, to anchor their own thought.

Recently, we began teaching *letter links* in conjunction with sign language at the High/Scope Demonstration Preschool, and the results have been fascinating. A *letter link* is a letter-linked picture of an object that starts with the same letter and sound as the child's first name; for example, a picture of a lion would be the letter link for Linus. (See p. 57 for more information about letter links.)

Teaching the manual alphabet along with the letter link system gives children another anchor to help them learn and retain the alphabet. Through this method, children are simultaneously learning the print form of the alphabet letter, the sound of the letter, and the sign for the letter. Adding the manual alphabet to the letter links provides a significant opportunity for enhancing children's visual acuity. It is a proactive, developmentally appropriate activity that engages a child's attention, and it trains the child to focus on the individual letters.

These are just a few suggestions and ideas you can do to incorporate the Head Start Domain Element of Literacy in your High/Scope daily routine. Always remember that your children are your best resources when planning any activity for them. Focus on their interests and developmental needs, and then you can add literacy and have a recipe for learning and fun for the children.

For more information on literacy activities, you may want to look at the many resource books available from High/Scope Press, including *Fee, Fie, Phonemic Awareness: 130 Prereading Activities for Preschoolers* by Mary Hohmann, *Preschool Readers and Writers: Early Literacy Strategies for Teachers* by Linda Ranweiler, *Letter Links: Alphabet Learning With Children's Names* by Andrea DeBruin-Parecki and Mary Hohmann, *Let's Talk Literacy: Practical Readings for Preschool Teachers,* edited by Mary Hohmann and Joanne Tangorra, *From Message to Meaning: Using a Daily Message Board in the Preschool Classroom* by Suzanne Gainsley, and *Storybook Talk: Conversations for Comprehension* by Mary Hohmann and Kate Adams.

Mathematics

Although mathematics is not one of the legislatively mandated outcomes in the Head Start Child Outcomes Framework, it is proving to be "the next big thing" in preschool. Here are some suggestions for covering the Domain Elements of Number and Operations, Geometry and Spatial Sense, and Patterns and Measurement:

Greeting Time

▼ Plan activities that include

– Counting how many children (how many girls, how many boys, etc.) are in school today.

– Having children count messages on the message board and make predictions about what they are going to do for the day.

– Having number and counting books available or books where children can compare sizes and shapes.

Large-Group Time

▼ Encourage children to name the positions they are in when doing movement and music activities.

▼ Sing counting songs and rhymes and play counting games.

▼ Have children make shapes with their bodies, trying it alone and then partnering with another child or a small group of children.

Small-Group Time

▼ Use a variety of manipulative items that can be counted, sorted, matched, sequenced, or put into a pattern.

▼ Include materials that can be taken apart and put together again.

▼ Plan activities that include opportunities for children to make observations about spatial relations of materials (e.g., *next to, in front of, behind, on top,* or *on bottom*).

Planning and Recall Times

▼ Have children tell you the first, second, and third things they will do or have done.

Planning small-group activities where children manipulate and sort different types of materials develops children's mathematical understandings.

▼ Use dice or number cards to determine who will recall or plan first, second, third, and so forth.

▼ Use a timer for recall to see how many things children can say about what happened before the timer runs out.

Mealtimes

▼ Use one-to-one correspondence when children are setting the table.

▼ Have the children determine a number of small snacks they will get beforehand and count out that number from the snack basket. For example, the children determine that each child will get four pretzels; they then count out that number from the snack basket. Children, of course, would be free to get more after they eat that number of pretzels (or whatever the snack is).

Naptime

▼ Have the children help you put out cots by counting how many you will need and naming the positions they are in.

▼ Use timers for naptime.

For more information on mathematic activities, you may want to look at the Teacher's Idea Book *"I'm Older Than You. I'm Five!" Math in the Preschool Classroom* by Ann S. Epstein and Suzanne Gainsley (High/Scope Press, 2005).

Head Start teachers who are using the High/Scope Curriculum can use the same process above to meet the other Domains or Head Start components. Just think about your specific children and your daily routine, and then you will be able to plan purposeful activities throughout the day that will stimulate your children.

Conducting Effective Small-Group Times

Small-group time serves as a wonderful tool for focusing on specific content, getting to know each child, and scaffolding early development on an individual as well as a group level. It is an adult-initiated learning experience based on children's interests and development. Depending on how many teachers you have in your classroom will determine how many small groups you will have — what is important is that the children are divided evenly among the teachers to form consistent groups. The child-adult ratio is important because small groups are a time when adults interact with individual children as well as the group as a whole, and children are also encouraged to interact with one another.

Small-Group Formation

Many Head Start teachers have questions about how to form the small groups in their classrooms, particularly which children to put in the same group. Since chil-

dren stay in the same group with the same adult for many months, if not the entire program year, these groupings are important. Although only you can be the final judge of what works best for the children in your setting, here are some questions you can ask yourself as you form small groups in your classroom:

▼ What are the personalities of the individual children? For example, are there children who are high energy, verbal, shy, quiet, independent, cautious, or curious? Strive for a mix in each group.

▼ What friendships/bonds among children already exist? Putting friends in the same group helps to encourage and extend these relationships. However, also make sure that children have a chance to share small-group experiences with those they may not otherwise play with.

▼ What bonds between the children and adults are already present from previous years in the program or through the community? Staying with familiar adults helps children develop a sense of security. However, it is also good for children to have experiences with a variety of adults and teaching styles, particularly since they will encounter new adults when they enter kindergarten. Judge on an individual basis whether a child will benefit most from continuity or a change at this point in time.

▼ Do any of the children have special needs, and what is the skill level of each adult or teacher to address these needs?

▼ Are any of the children English language learners, and what is the fluency of staff in the language(s) children speak?

▼ What are the ages and gender of children in your classroom? Strive for a mix in each group.

In answering these questions, you can find out how to group children in a way that

Keeping consistent small groups throughout the year helps this teacher plan for the children's developmental needs.

is best for you and your children. Once you group your children into small groups, it is imperative to stay with that same consistent group. This helps teachers get to know children on an individual basis and to plan for their developmental needs as small groups share planning and recall together. (In many programs, children also eat with their small groups, which provides another experience in which they can extend their language as well as social and fine motor skills in a familiar and secure environment.)

Many Head Start teachers are concerned about not being able to have small-group time with all of their children or feel a need to have all the children in their small group at least for some part of the year. In cases like this, you can switch your groups halfway through the year, such as in January when

everyone returns from winter break. Alternatively, if you have two teachers, you can switch three children at a time to each group every nine weeks. By the third nine-week period, you will end up with your team teacher's original group and she will end up with yours.

Purpose of Small-Group Time

Other questions about small-group time center around the content of what is to happen at small groups. The activities for small-group time stem from these four sources:

▼ Children's interests

▼ Curriculum content (Head Start Child Outcomes, key developmental indicators, [KDIs], Child Observation Record [COR] items, or your state standards)

▼ New, unexplored, or underused materials in the classroom

▼ Local traditions or community events

Small-group time is designed for teachers to have individual time with each child and to be able to better assess each child's needs to plan for each child's developmental progress. Because of the push for academics in preschool, sometimes teachers have a tendency of trying to make the small-group-time activity one that is of the directive nature to teach a lesson or academic skill. Some people in the Head Start community think that High/Scope is against teaching academic skills. There is nothing wrong with teaching academics in High/Scope preschool classrooms, but there is a way to do it that is not of a directive nature. There are studies that show the advantages of child-initiated over adult-directed instruction for children's short- and long-term development. For example, long-term studies of young people who were enrolled in a High/Scope preschool program compared to a direct instruction curriculum show they were involved in fewer delinquent acts as adolescents and commit fewer crimes as adults (Schweinhart, Weikart, & Larner, 1986). Corroborating research in non-High/Scope settings comes from other researchers (Burts et al., 1992; Marcon, 2002).

Learning at Small-Group Time

During small-group time, children contribute their own ideas, participate at their own developmental levels, and have their own set of materials to explore and use in their own way. Small-group time should be a fun activity as well as a learning activity. The learning occurs when you, the teacher, introduce the activity and then move from child to child to interact with and see how each child uses the materials and interprets the activity. When you use the following small-group-time interaction strategies with each individual child, learning will occur:

▼ Observe what the child is doing and how he or she is using the materials.

▼ Comment on what the child is doing and saying.

▼ Imitate and add to the child's actions.

▼ Use the materials in the same way the child is using them.

▼ Extend what the child is doing.

The last strategy requires thinking on your feet and planning in advance — figuring out on the spot how you can extend the child's actions and connect learning to it. You may have a focus in mind for your small group, but planning in advance as well as thinking about the children's developmental range enables you to think of what other strategies can be used based on how the children will respond to the materials or the activity itself. For example, one Head Start teacher planned a small-group activity with the counting bears; her focus was patterning by sizes. She started her small group with her opening statement:

> Today for small group I have some bears that are different sizes. See the family pattern I'm making: large, medium, small. I'm wondering what kinds of patterns you can make with your bears?

The teacher then turned the materials over to the children and observed how they were using them. One child began grouping his bears by color; another child counted her bears. Two children began using their bears as puppets, role-playing and giving them funny voices to talk with. Three children were playing a racing game of who could match their bears to the sizes the fastest. Two children were actually doing what the teacher said in her opening statement about sizes of the bears and the patterns. This High/Scope-trained Head Start teacher moved from child to child and interacted with them using the strategies listed previously and built on their interactions with the materials. With the child that was grouping his bears by color, she made comments on what he was doing, saying, "You've grouped all your bears by their colors. I'm going to try that, too." She also talked with him about the different colors he was using. She extended the activity by saying, "I wonder how else we could group the bears?" She paused, giving the child a chance to respond, and then said "Let's try grouping them by sizes. Let's do it together."

Moving onto the next child in her small group, the teacher began counting her bears like the child who was counting hers. She compared her number with the child's number and talked about who had more bears and who had less: "I wonder how many large-size bears we both have? Let's count just the large-size bears together." She asked

her to continue on with the medium and small ones, as she moved to the next two children who were role-playing with their bears. She picked up a bear that was a contrasting size of the ones they were using and begin giving it a voice, saying, "Hi there. I am a medium-sized bear and I like to eat medium-sized cookies. What size bear are you and what size cookies do you like to eat?"

With the children who were racing with their bears, she joined in on the racing game and said, "I wonder if we can race to see who can group the small bears first?" Then she did the same with the large and medium bears. These are just some examples of how one teacher extended the activities that the children chose while adding learning to her original idea in her opening statement.

Although you begin your small-group times with an opening statement and an idea

If small-group time comes right before planning time, children can continue to use the materials. These two children extend the small-group activity on blowing leaves with straws to using the straws in another area during work time.

in mind, don't be surprised if children in your group use the materials you give them in a totally different way than you had in mind, as shown by the counting bears activity that this Head Start teacher had planned. This can be a good thing, because the children are letting you know where they are developmentally and where their interests lie. It can also help you better plan for them by observing what they do as you interact with them on their level using strategies previously stated and enjoying the experience.

Placement of Small-Group Time

Another issue concerning small-group time is the placement of it in the daily routine. As stated before, your daily routine has to work for you and the children in your setting. High/Scope cannot tell you how and where to place your components; we only ask that you keep the plan-do-review sequence intact. Some Head Start teachers put their small-group time right before the planning time. When that occurs, children usually finish their small-group time activity (and are therefore already gathered together in their group with the adult) and the teacher plans with individual children (for ideas on planning time, see the Teacher's Idea Book, *Making the Most of Plan-Do-Review* by Nancy Vogel [High/Scope Press, 2001]). Children then make their plans and proceed to work time. This gives them the option of continuing to use the materials and extend their activities from small-group time into work time. If their plans are in other areas of the room or with different materials, they would put away their small-group materials before beginning to carry out their work time.

A main concern with having planning time following small-group time is that effective planning strategies can get lost in the shuffle. Since children will finish small-group activities at different times, it is important to make sure you have a planning strategy planned that children can carry out with you.

Including Families in the Program

The parent involvement component is a vital part to the organization of the Head Start program on all levels, from the classroom to the administrative level as well as from the city to the state to the national level. The Head Start Bureau reported that in the 2004–2005 program year more than 890,000 current or former parents volunteered in Head Start classrooms (National Head Start Association, 2006). Parent involvement is also mandated in the HSPPS. The standards require each program to

▼ Build relationships with the families of the enrolled children as early as possible to create ongoing opportunities for parental involvement throughout the time their children are in the program.

▼ Help families work toward their goals by linking them to the necessary services that will assist them in reaching their goals.

▼ Open the program to parents at any time, involving them in the development of program curriculum, with opportunities to volunteer.

▼ Involve parents in program decision making and governance.

▼ Provide parents with opportunities to enhance their parenting skills. (HSPPS, 2006)

These standards were designed to help build stronger families and values among the Head Start community. To strengthen the role of fathers in families, Head Start launched the Fatherhood Initiative. To reinforce its support of families even further, Head Start recently began the Healthy Marriage Initiative to help couples who have chosen marriage to form and sustain a healthy marriage (DHHS, 2007b).

Just like Head Start, High/Scope has recognized that a parent is the child's first and best educator, which is why High/Scope takes parent involvement seriously also. The High/Scope Curriculum is guided by the plan-do-review process and the principals of intrinsic motivation. High/Scope encourages sharing of child observations for assessment, emphasizes materials and activities that originate in the child's home (not toy kits brought from outside), focuses on improving adult interaction, and encourages teachers to create partnerships with parents.

Introducing Parents to the High/Scope Curriculum

Entry into Head Start may be the first time that a child and parent are spending a significant portion of the day apart. It is often a young child's first learning experience outside the home. This can be both an exciting and somewhat scary time for adults and children. Parents, in particular, may wonder whether the curriculum used in their child's program is consistent with their goals for what and how their child learns. Many parents who enroll their children in Head Start are not familiar with the High/Scope Curriculum and its principles. Informing the parents how their children will learn with the High/Scope Curriculum will make them feel more comfortable as well as confident that they have made the best choice for their child by enrolling them in your program.

The best way to introduce parents to the High/Scope Curriculum is to do it at the onset of your program. Hosting an open house is a fun way to accomplish this, where parents experience the High/Scope's daily

Both Head Start and High/Scope recognize that a parent is a child's first and best educator and strongly promote parental involvement in the classroom.

routine in a modified fashion. They can begin the open house with greeting time with a message board that will list all the daily routine activities that they will experience during the open house, so they can see what their children experience in a Head Start–High/Scope classroom. Have them tour the room's areas and materials, and go through a short plan-do-review sequence. You can also conduct a brief small- and large-group time or show videotapes about what and how children learn in a High/Scope classroom (for a list of videotape and other resources you can use in teacher-training and parent workshops, see Appendix B).

Other ways to inform the parents about the High/Scope Curriculum is to hold workshops either before, during, or after parent meetings. The parent meetings are held monthly as mandated by the HSPPS, making it a natural way to inform parents about the curriculum. Workshops for parents do not have to be as long as staff training workshops — just enough time for parents to become actively involved and have more understanding of how the curriculum benefits their child. The Teacher's Idea Book *The Essential Parent Workshop Resource,* by Michelle Graves (High/Scope Press, 2000), is filled with 30 one-hour workshop plans and agendas for parents to learn about the High/Scope Curriculum.

Encouraging Parental Involvement

Perhaps the most important thing parents can do to improve the quality of care their child receives is to be involved. Again, because of the Welfare to Work program, many Head Start parents became working parents. This made it somewhat difficult for some parents to volunteer in the classroom or attend parent meetings.

Here are some alternative suggestions to encourage parents to become involved in your programs:

▼ Communicate with a child's family about what the child has done during the day. If possible, the child's primary teacher should talk with the parents, but you can also share information through daily news sheets and observations. At departure time, the child's primary teacher can also reconfirm the next time the child will be back, and, if possible, let the parent and child know some of the things that will be happening in the program on that day.

▼ Include busy parents in the program day — even in small ways during arrival and departure times. Use conversations, handouts, e-mail messages, and open houses to educate parents and other family members on how they can extend the child's education at home.

▼ Plan your parent meetings and special events during times when most parents can attend. Survey your parents to see when they can come and make sure you accommodate those available times at least sometime during your program year. An added benefit would be to offer child care services if you plan something for the parents after school hours. Transportation (a program van, coordinating car pools, and vouchers for public transportation) may also facilitate attendance by removing some of the barriers that would prevent parents from participating. Serving food is always a big draw, so parents don't have to worry about choosing between coming to the meeting or preparing dinner for their family.

▼ Take a look at the parent interest survey that each parent completes during the Head Start enrollment process, and make a list of the things your parents are interested in. Just like High/Scope teachers plan activities and events based on the children's interests, the same can be done

How Parents Can Be Involved

Newsletter

Personal notes

Activity calendars

Parent handbooks

Notebook communication

Parent meetings

Workshops

Parent/teacher conferences

Training courses (GED, CDA, etc.)

Advisory board or committee

Book study group

Invitations to attend professional meetings

Family literacy program

Parent support groups

Family night

Pot lucks and picnics

Home visits by teachers

Parent-to-parent home visits

Videotaping of teacher

Classroom volunteers

Making observations of children

Sharing a talent

Field trips

Orientation visits

Visiting other centers/schools

Parent bulletin boards

Parent library

Toy lending library

Parents' room

Getting books from library

Making story tapes

Making furniture or materials

Making labels, assisting in room setup

Helping with classroom repairs

Assessing classroom with PQA

Helping to build the playground

Playground assessment

Contributing snacks

Fundraising

Suggestion box

Children's interest file

Establishing links with agencies

Making phone calls

Donating materials

Informal contact/conversations

for the children's parents by using their interest surveys.

▼ Acknowledge the need to accommodate families from different cultures — many families believe that school is the teacher's (the expert's) domain and do not want to be involved in any way. If that is the case, this needs to be respected. Some family members may have less facility with English than the child who attends the program. With that in mind, it may be necessary to also accommodate family members who are not literate or are English language learners.

Offering choices is central to High/Scope's philosophy of working with children, and the same philosophy should extend to parents — especially if you are trying to promote parent involvement. Parent involvement can take many forms, and adults in Head Start programs should accept

When involving parents in the classroom, it is important to consider (and take advantage of) the wealth of diversity the children bring to the class.

this variety. One parent may wish to have a phone conversation with the teacher once a month; another may come in for her child's birthday.

Parents may resist involvement with the school for many reasons: They may have had negative school experiences as children, they may feel they are too busy, or they may be consumed by job or family stress. Even with these problems, adults are more likely to be involved if they are intrinsically motivated to participate. Thus, if we want parents to participate, we should plan all parent involvement and support activities around the factors of intrinsic motivation. The likelihood of sustained parent involvement and support will increase if parents enjoy their involvement, have choices, do things that interest them, and feel successful and competent in their efforts.

To communicate to parents that their level of involvement with the school is a matter of choice, distribute a list with some of the ideas of connecting with parents (see the sidebar on p. 41). Staff and parents can then develop the parent involvement aspect of the program collectively.

These are some suggestions for connecting with parents and involving them in your program. Remember that your Head Start parent involvement coordinator or content area specialist is available to assist you in this as well. Your family service worker, who most often makes the first contact with the parent in the Head Start program, can also help you.

Collaborating Effectively With Other Adults
Daily Team Planning

Daily team planning is a big challenge for many Head Start programs using the High/Scope Curriculum. This is the time of day when the teaching team members in the same classroom come together and review

Taking time to review the day's events and plan for the next day as a team is essential in meeting the full range of children's needs.

the day they had with the children by discussing their child observations (anecdotes) and ways to support individual children by planning activities for the following day. Activities based on children's interests, gleaned from thoughtful observations, allow each child to receive the daily individual attention he or she deserves. Daily team planning is a key component in meeting the full range of children's needs. Therefore, it is important to find time when the teachers in your Head Start program can meet to share their observations and develop plans for the upcoming day.

Typically, in a full-day program, the teaching team will get together when the children are napping. In a half-day program, they usually convene in between sessions and/or at the end of the day when the afternoon children leave. During daily team planning, teachers compare observations and enter them into the COR. In developing new plans, teachers will fill out the daily lesson plan form used by their center. These new plans are posted as teachers complete them or by the day's end. The idea is that parents and staff sho ld be able to see the plans before the actual activities takc place.

Marlon and Tower Building

It is work time on a Monday and four-year-old Marlon expresses an interest in tower making with the small, colored blocks in the toy area. The teacher begins to interact with him and notices that although he is very much into building with the blocks, he is not really paying particular interest in the patterns of the colors or sizes that he is making his tower in. The teacher uses a few scaffolding techniques to try to extend that but stops when she realizes that Marlon is much more content and pleased with the building of the tower. The teacher quickly makes a brief anecdote of this interaction and continues interacting and playing with Marlon following his leads.

At day's end during team planning with the coteacher, she shares this anecdote as well as the interactions that took place with her and Marlon. Together the teachers plan a small group to occur tomorrow (on Tuesday) for Marlon's group to build "tower patterns" with the same colored blocks that Marlon was using today. How wonderful for Marlon to get his need met and acted upon the very next day! His interest in tower building is still fresh and exciting to him, but will it still be next week if his teachers were forced to plan their lessons weekly and would have had to plan that lesson for next Monday, seven days from the time when he first expressed interest? What about other teachable moments that happens in the classroom throughout the daily routine? How will they be captured in the moment of learning, meeting the child where he or she is, and expanding upon it immediately or, at least, the very next day?

The research tells us that intrinsic motivation is what causes lasting and long-term effects for children's success in school. If lesson plans are made based on children's interests, developmental levels, Head Start Child Outcomes, KDIs or COR items, then teachers need to plan them on a daily basis to ensure that children are making the connections in the above areas and that they are meeting the needs of the children on a daily basis.

Some issues of daily team planning in Head Start programs include (1) finding time to actually sit down and do it and (2) having the support of the administrative team to allow team planning to occur daily and not requiring teaching staff to complete and submit weekly or monthly lesson plans.

This second challenge is a very important issue. It stems mainly from administrators not knowing or realizing the importance and benefits of daily team planning — through daily team planning, teachers can immediately respond with an activity or support strategy to the need of a child the very next day. This is crucial when you are using the High/Scope Curriculum, which bases much of its planning around the children's interests and expressed ideas. See the sidebar on Marlon and tower building for an example on how daily team planning enables teachers to find those teachable moments.

As the author of this book and a former Head Start teacher, I would like to share my story about daily team planning. Before the Head Start center that I worked for adopted the High/Scope Curriculum, the teachers at my center did weekly lesson plans. Every Friday I would sit in my classroom with my coteacher and write five lesson plans for the upcoming week, trying to remember what **I** did this time last year when **I** had this theme. What materials do **I** have that would support this theme? What do **I** want the children to know about this theme? How many ways can **I** instruct my children in order for them to learn this theme? What type of bulletin board can **I** put up to let parents and administrators know what theme **I'm** working on?

I was not happy with this system, to the point of feeling ill every Friday afternoon. The planning had no connection with the children I was serving. It was about me, the teacher, and all my questions began with "I." How could I, instead, plan with the children in mind, based on their interests and developmental needs?

I finally received an answer to my question at a High/Scope training done at my Head Start agency and breathed a huge sigh of relief when I actually realized what daily team planning meant. It was easy as a, b, c. I could (a) play and interact with the children in my classroom throughout the day; (b) take observational notes on their interests, strengths, and needs; and then (c) at the end of the day, sit down with my coteacher and have a conversation about these observations of the children and discuss what activities and strategies we could do tomorrow to support them. These would be written down on the lesson plan form and posted. I was gratified to see how this type of daily team planning meant children in my classroom received lessons based on them and not based on me, lessons that I, as a teacher, knew would stay with them long after they left my classroom. Because my coteacher and I took the time every day to plan these lessons based on the children's intrinsic motivation and developmental needs, the learning was authentic, meaningful, and lasting.

Once teachers get into the routine of planning this way, it feels natural and proceeds efficiently. However, Head Start teachers are often concerned at first that they will not be able to fit this into their daily schedules, that making ongoing observations will disrupt the flow of the day, or that going through the team sharing and planning process will be time consuming. Here are some suggestions to facilitate daily team planning that have worked in the past with Head Start programs using the High/Scope Curriculum:

▼ **Make a board in the classroom where teachers can jot down notes that they think of during the day** and would like to remember for tomorrow's lesson plan.

Use sticky notes or a pocket planner. This is very useful for teaching teams who physically cannot sit down with each other to team plan, due to conflicting work schedules or time constraints. Using a board like this can help the communication process. Teachers can take turns to write the daily lesson plans by using the notes placed on the board by the other teacher who may have had to leave earlier. By using e-mail or phones for clarification and checking-in purposes, the teacher who is compiling the next day's lesson can communicate with the other before making the plan and have it posted in the morning for all to see. This strategy can be modified to fit your setting and situation at your Head Start program. The main focus here is communication among the team members. Once you decide that this is something you want to do, you must do whatever it takes to get it done — be creative in making it work.

▼ **Solicit the assistance of other adults in the program that are in non-teaching roles to be with children while teaching team members plan.** This strategy was adopted by the administrative staff at The Order of the Fishermen Ministry Head Start program in Detroit, Michigan. The administrative staff, from the director on down, made a firm decision to support the teaching staff so that the teachers could better support the children. To send this support message in a clear and concrete way, administrative staff members were assigned to center staff to physically be with the Head Start children while the teachers planned, at the end of each half-day session, at the end of a full-day session, or during naptime, whatever worked best for the teachers. Again, Head Start programs can tailor this suggestion to fit their individual needs. What it takes is a decision from all the staff to work together to find the best solution to make the daily team planning a reality. Doing so will be much more rewarding for the teaching staff and the program as a whole, but, most important, for the children and families you serve.

Partnering With the Community

Head Start programs are required to establish community partnerships with agencies in their community to help further expand the services that they offer to children and families. These partnerships can include elaborate setups, such as a dental office coming to the center to give dental checkups to the Head Start children and their families, to the most simplest relationship with the corner grocery store to donate boxes and other discarded materials for the Head Start classrooms.

Day care center collaborations have become increasingly popular among Head Start programs as a result of the Welfare to Work program and the need to provide full-day (sometimes called wraparound) services to children and families. In this kind of collaboration, a Head Start program seeks out a day care center in its service area to form a collaboration in which both agencies benefit. The Head Start program benefits because it is able to count any child who meets the required qualifications of the Head Start program as part of its enrollment. The day care center benefits because it will be entitled to all the services that Head Start offers that the day care center may not be able to financially afford. If a day care center is fortunate enough to collaborate with a Head Start program using the High/Scope Curriculum, then the center also benefits by receiving a high-quality curriculum with training from the Head Start staff who have been trained in the curriculum. The day care center also receives Head Start staff, who are paid by Head Start to work in the classroom with the children who are eligible. This gives the day care center extra staff to provide more services to their children and families. All in all it is a win-win situation for both parties involved.

Thinking About Your Program

In this chapter we have explored issues that are of particular concern to Head Start programs using the High/Scope Curriculum: planning a flexible daily routine, connecting the Head Start content areas and Domains with the High/Scope Curriculum, conducting effective small-group times, including families in your program, and collaborating effectively with other adults in the program and the community.

How will you apply what you are learning to your own program? What new questions do you have? As you think about these questions, take a look at the sample daily routines in Chapter 3 and the questions posed by other Head Start personnel in Chapter 4. Be sure to see Appendix B for related reading on other topics discussed in this and other chapters.

3

Sample Daily Routines: Head Start Preschool Programs

very Head Start program has unique features that staff need to keep in mind when designing a daily routine. Looking at other programs' routines can help stimulate your creativity in developing a daily routine that you will be able to keep consistent yet flexible. Consider the two sample routines below.

Daily Routine #1

The Order of the Fishermen Ministry Head Start Program, Detroit, Michigan

The Order of the Fishermen Ministry (TOFM) Head Start has six centers, including one High/Scope-accredited center, and three collaboration sites (with Head Start classrooms in them). In the High/Scope-accredited center, there is at least one High/Scope certified teacher in every classroom, and the center has an ongoing relationship with a High/Scope certified trainer. The center has also been evaluated by High/Scope and passed rigorous criteria for curriculum implementation, professional development, and program management. (For information on High/Scope teacher

and trainer certification and program accreditation, click on Certification on the Training & Conferences page at *www.highscope.org*).

Number of children: 51 (three classrooms; one is self-contained and the other two are in an open area [with no walls or dividers to separate them] but operate as separate classes)

Ages of children: 3–5 years

Number of staff: Six teachers, one family service worker, and one cook who is housed at another center across the street but cooks for both centers

Child arrival and departure times: 8:30 a.m.–4:30 p.m. (full day)

Teachers' work hours: 8:00 a.m.–5:00 p.m., Mon.–Thur.; 8:00 a.m.–12:00 noon, Fridays = 40-hour work week

8:30–8:45 a.m. Arrival/Greeting time

This is the time when all the children arrive at the center. One teacher stands at the door to greet the parents and children upon arrival while the other teacher is sitting on the rug in the classroom ready to receive the children with books,

small plastic building blocks, or puzzles, depending on what the teachers' plans are. The teacher at the door also assists the children with the signing-in process to show that they are present in school today. At around 8:40 the teacher at the door joins the children on the rug, and both teachers and children start the day with a good morning song. The teachers direct the children's attention to the message board, and together they read the messages, which will include selecting children to be on the helper chart, picking two children to choose songs to be sung at large-group time, and any other happenings that are pertinent to the children on that day. After greeting time is over, children transition to the breakfast area to prepare for breakfast.

8:45–9:15 a.m. Breakfast preparation/ Breakfast/Tooth brushing

During this time the children wash their hands and set the table for breakfast. Usually every child is busy with a job, whether it is bathroom captain (makes sure the children throw away disposable cups and paper towels and that the soap and paper supplies are in place before and after tooth brushing), table setter, milk captain (gets the milk out of the refrigerator kept in the office), or daily routine captain (moves arrow along the posted pictorial daily routine) — the teachers and children are working together. As children finish their breakfast, they leave the table and go directly to the bathroom (which is inside the classroom) to brush their teeth. After they have brushed their teeth, the children go to the meeting area and sit and read or talk quietly as the others come over. When the majority of the children are in the meeting area, one teacher will begin large-group time with an easy-to-join activity so other children who are

At The Order of the Fishermen Ministry (TOFM) Head Start, children actively participate in breakfast preparation. These two children are responsible for bringing the milk to the eating area.

still brushing their teeth can join at any time.

9:15–9:40 a.m. Large-group time

The two children who were picked at greeting time choose a song for the class to sing out of the song book (a collection of songs that the children know and love to sing) — this is sometimes done during the transition before large group starts to save time. After singing, the children and the adults participate in the large-group-time activity that the teachers planned based on the children's interests, a content area in physical development or the arts, a cooperative play project, or an event currently meaningful to the children. The children then move to the tables for small-group time using a teacher-planned transition activity.

Both TOFM teachers actively participate in this large-group-time activity that involves movement and music.

9:40–9:55 a.m. Small-group time

Each teacher and her group of 8 or 9 children (there are 17 children in each classroom) convene at their perspective small-group tables. Once the children finish small-group time, they clean up and then stay in the same groups to plan.

9:55–10:00 a.m. Planning time

The children meet in their groups for planning time and share their plans for the morning by using a planning strategy that the teachers have prepared beforehand and that is based on some children's interests, developmental abilities, or a content area.

10:00–11:00 a.m. Work time

Children carry out their plans and may make new plans. As in any work time, both teachers are actively supporting the children in play.

11:00–11:10 a.m. Cleanup time

Children return materials to the appropriate interest areas in the classroom. The cleanup captain gives a five-minute warning to all the children. After five minutes, the cleanup captain turns out the lights, which signals the children to begin singing a cleanup song and cleaning the room. The teachers use a variety of cleanup strategies, such as the "Freeze Song" (everyone cleans up while the music plays; when an adult stops the music, everyone freezes until the adult says, "Find another toy to put away" and then begins the music again), Beat the Timer, and How Many Songs till Cleanup.

11:10–11:15 a.m. Recall time

The children meet back in their groups for recall time and share their experiences of the morning by using a recall strategy planned by the teachers based on some children's interests, developmental abilities, or a content area.

11:15–11:30 a.m. Story time/Hand washing/Lunch preparation

The two groups are still in their separate groups at this time. The teachers read a selected story, and one selected child reads a book of his or her choice in the class's "author's chair." This book can be selected from the class library or brought from home. The children and teachers then wash their hands and prepare for lunch. The same helpers from the helper chart do their current jobs again.

11:30 a.m.–12:00 noon Family-style lunch

Lunch is served according to the Child and Adult Care Food Program (CACFP) guidelines. The teachers and children also enjoy relaxing mealtime conversation at this time.

12:00 noon–12:30 p.m. Preparation for naptime

As children finish their lunch, they clean up, go to the bathroom, and prepare themselves for naptime by getting their blankets and pillows and assisting the teachers with setting up the cots.

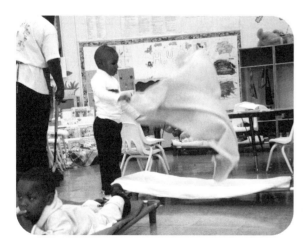

Children learn self-help skills at TOFM as they help prepare their cots for naptime.

12:30–2:30 p.m. Naptime/Teachers' lunch/Daily team planning

Most children fall fast asleep, but some who are not nappers lay quietly on their cots; explore books; or play with small, soft toys (like stuffed animals) on their cots. All three classrooms nap together and at the same time so that the teachers can take their lunch hour (12:00–1:00 first set takes lunch; second set takes lunch from 1:00–2:00). Daily team planning occurs for everyone from 2:00–2:30 in the classroom.

2:30–2:45 p.m. Wakeup/Cleanup from nap

Lights are turned on at 2:30, and the children begin waking. They go to the bathroom, put their bedding away, and assist the teachers with putting away the cots.

2:45–3:00 p.m. Journal writing

This is the time of day when children have the opportunity to write or draw anything they want about what happened in school today. At this time, teachers are interacting with children as if it were a writing activity at small-group time. Sometimes teachers will give children a topic to write about.

3:00–3:45 p.m. Outside time

The playground for this center happens to be across a major street with five lanes of heavy traffic to cross. Yet, this center goes out outside everyday to the playground if weather permits. The adults and children practice traffic safety by crossing at the corner traffic light. An adult holds a handheld stop sign (purchased by the center) because 51 children and 6 adults don't always make it across before the green light turns to red — the traffic waits patiently for the last child to cross.

Daily Routine #1 At-A-Glance

8:30–8:45 a.m.	Arrival/Greeting time	11:30 a.m.–12:00 noon	Family-style lunch
8:45–9:15 a.m.	Breakfast preparation/Breakfast/Tooth brushing	12:00 noon–12:30 p.m.	Preparation for naptime
9:15–9:40 a.m.	Large-group time	12:30–2:30 p.m.	Naptime/Teachers' lunch/Daily team planning
9:40–9:55 a.m.	Small-group time	2:30–2:45 p.m.	Wakeup/Cleanup from nap
9:55–10:00 a.m.	Planning time	2:45–3:00 p.m.	Journal writing
10:00–11:00 a.m.	Work time	3:00–3:45 p.m.	Outside time
11:00–11:10 a.m.	Cleanup time	3:45–4:00 p.m.	Free reading/Story time
11:10–11:15 a.m.	Recall time	4:00–4:30 p.m.	Snacktime/Departure/Cleanup
11:15–11:30 a.m.	Story time/Hand washing/Lunch preparation		

At the playground there is stationary equipment, including climbers, a slide, and rocking horses on springs. Earlier in the morning, between 8–8:30, an adult had brought portable equipment (e.g., tricycles, balls, hoops, and so forth) over to the locked parking lot across the street from the playground so that adults can easily take them out for the children to play with.

3:45–4:00 p.m. Free reading/Story time

After the children return from outside time, reading time begins. This time children sit together on the large-group rug and choose books to read to each other or with a friend. This is more of a shared reading time. Sometimes children choose to do another author's chair, but it would be to a small group of children who were interested.

4:00–4:30 p.m. Snacktime/Departure/Cleanup

After the free reading and story time, children and teachers prepare for snack by washing their hands, setting the table, and putting out food. Sometimes the children participate in making the snack if it is a cooking or nutrition activity planned by the teachers and based on the children's interest or the content area of nutrition. In this particular program, pickups start at about 4:15; however, the big rush is usually around 4:30, which is the time that ends the day for children and parents. The staff leaves at 5:00. From 4:30–5:00, they clean up and prepare for tomorrow's session, which begins at 8:00 so they can prepare for the Head Start children to arrive at 8:30 and repeat the daily routine again.

Daily Routine #2
Adrian Head Start Comstock Center, Adrian, Michigan
Half-Day Session

Number of children: 126 (five classrooms: three full-day classrooms and two half-day classrooms); the classroom described here has two teachers and 18 children (9 children in each group)

Ages of children: 3–5 years

Number of staff: 14 (10 teachers, one secretary, one center manager, and two family support coordinators)

Child arrival and departure times: 6:00 a.m.–12:30 p.m., Mon.–Fri.

Teachers' work hours: 6:00 a.m.–2:00 p.m., Mon.–Fri. = 40-hour work week

6:15–8:15 a.m. Arrival time/Snacktime

For the first two hours most of the children coming in are still asleep; their parents take them right to their prepared cots to continue sleeping. There is an open snack available for those who want to eat. Then half of the room is open for table toys, books, art, and computers.

8:15–8:45 a.m. Breakfast preparation

This program participates in the CACFP, so the children wash their hands and set the tables for breakfast. The food is sent in from the Adrian Public Schools District.

8:45–9:00 a.m. Cleanup from breakfast/Tooth brushing

This classroom has a bathroom inside the classroom and also a sink. As children finish their breakfast, they clean up and go brush their teeth. Then they go to the classroom rug to read a book until greeting time.

At the Adrian Head Start Comstock Center, one teacher uses the children's interest in pumpkins at Halloween to create a small-group activity that involves all the senses.

9:00–9:15 a.m. Greeting time/Large-group time

Teachers and children read the message board and go right into large-group time, which consists of movement and music activities. Teachers then transition children to their small-group tables with a planned transition activity.

9:15–9:30 a.m. Small-group time

Each teacher has nine children, and each teacher introduces a planned activity based on the interests and developmental abilities of the children in their group. At the end of small-group time, children clean up.

Teachers often use simple props for recall time. This Adrian Head Start teacher is using finger puppets to encourage each child to share what he or she did during work time.

9:30–9:40 a.m. Planning time

Children plan their work-time experiences; they share their plans by using a planning strategy prepared by the teacher based on children's interests, developmental abilities, or a content area.

9:40–10:40 a.m. Work time

Children carry out their plans and may make new plans. Both teachers are actively supporting the children in play.

10:40–10:50 a.m. Cleanup time

There is a five-minute warning for when work time will end. A selected child will go around the room displaying a red hand with a number 5 on it telling children, "Five more minutes until cleanup time." After five minutes, the same child takes the green hand and announces, "It's cleanup time." The teachers use a variety of cleanup strategies for this time.

10:50–11:00 a.m. Recall time

The children meet back in their small groups for recall time and share their experiences of the morning by using a recall strategy planned by each teacher based on some children's interests, developmental abilities, or a content area.

11:00–11:30 a.m. Outside time

This center has a fenced-in playground with ample space and stationary play equipment, including swing sets, a slide, a sand box, and sand toys. Bikes and other portable outside toys are housed in the outside storage shed located on the playground.

11:30–11:45 a.m. Lunch preparation

All children participate in preparing for lunch by washing their hands and setting the tables.

Daily Routine #2 At-A-Glance

6:15–8:15 a.m.	Arrival time/Snack-time	9:40–10:40 a.m.	Work time
8:15–8:45 a.m.	Breakfast preparation	10:40–10:50 a.m.	Cleanup time
		10:50–11:00 a.m.	Recall time
8:45–9:00 a.m.	Cleanup from breakfast/Tooth brushing	11:00–11:30 a.m.	Outside time
		11:30–11:45 a.m.	Lunch preparation
9:00–9:15 a.m.	Greeting time/Large-group time	11:45 a.m.–12:15 p.m.	Family-style lunch
		12:15–12:30 p.m.	Books/Dismissal
9:15–9:30 a.m.	Small-group time	12:30–1:00 p.m.	Daily team planning
9:30–9:40 a.m.	Planning time		

11:45 a.m.–12:15 p.m. Family-style lunch

Lunch is served according to the CACFP guidelines. Both teachers and children enjoy relaxing mealtime conversation at this time. As children finish their lunch, they clean up and go to the rug for book reading.

12:15–12:30 p.m. Books/Dismissal

Children read books and converse with their classmates and teachers while they wait for their parents to pick them up. Some children transition at this time to the afternoon program that is offered by the YWCA in the same building.

12:30–1:00 p.m. Daily team planning

Both teachers participate in daily team planning. They also enter their daily anecdotes into the computerized Child Observation Record (COR) program. They clean up the classroom; their work day ends at 2:00 p.m.

4

Questions and Answers About Head Start Preschool Programs

no doubt you have many questions about the ins and outs of implementing the High/Scope Curriculum in a Head Start Preschool program. You are not alone! In this chapter, you will read the questions and concerns of other Head Start teachers, parents, and administrative staff. The answers are based on the Head Start experience of the author and other High/Scope practitioners working in Head Start settings.

Learning Environment

I am new Head Start teacher, and I just started working at a center that uses the High/Scope Curriculum. I was eager to decorate my classroom for the first day of school and hung up a brand-new, store-bought alphabet train on the wall. My center administrator looked in my room and told me that High/Scope does not encourage teachers to post store-bought alphabets on the wall. Can you tell me why?

Given that your purpose in posting the alphabet is so the children in your classroom learn their letters, there are more effective (and less expensive) ways to accomplish this goal. Children rarely refer to those posted, decoration-type alphabet posters or hangings as a reference to learn the alphabet, especially if they are posted above their eye level. Since the High/Scope Curriculum is centered on active participatory learning, you will want to have alphabet letters in your classroom that children can handle (hold, touch, trace, copy), examine up close, and combine with other materials. This way they can make discoveries through direct hands-on and minds-on contact with the alphabet. This also saves the wall space to post and display things that the children have made themselves.

Materials to invest in that will lend themselves to this active participatory learning would include:

▼ Sets of colorful, plastic magnetic letters

▼ Large wooden letters that can be held and traced

▼ Sponge letters to be used with painting or water play

▼ Movable alphabet letter sets that are in many different sizes

▼ Laminated cardboard or corrugated letter sets

▼ Letter stamps to be used with ink pads or paints

▼ Letter beads that can be strung to make necklaces or bracelets or in other ways the children want to use them

▼ Alphabet cookie cutters to be used for play dough, clay, and so forth

▼ Different textured letters, such as those made from soft-pillow-type materials, velvet, or coarse paper

▼ Alphabet pretzels, cereal, and crackers to be eaten at snacktime

Two of the Head Start Indicators from the Child Outcomes state that each child:

• Identifies at least 10 letters of the alphabet, especially those in their own name.

• Knows that letters of the alphabet are a special category of visual graphics that can be individually named. (U.S. Department of Health and Human Services, 2003)

Many teachers try to meet those Indicators by drilling individual letters (e.g., the "letter of the day") and teaching the alphabet song. The alphabet song only teaches children a song; they don't learn their letters, they learn a tune — how many times have you heard that famous new alphabet letter, "elemeno"? High/Scope's goal for children learning the alphabet is for letters to be meaningful and for children to understand how the alphabet is used in reading and writing. Put another

Movable alphabet letter sets, magnetic letters, sponge letters, cookie-cutter letters, and corrugated letter sets are all materials that children can manipulate and lend themselves to active participatory learning.

way, the reason to learn letters is because they have a useful function in communication. Promoting meaningful letter learning is best accomplished by surrounding children with many real examples of print in their learning environment, not drilling them in isolated letters. This includes labeling materials and having text that holds meaning and value for the children's immediate community. It also means having books (specifically alphabet books), magazines, menus, calendars, and phone books in the classroom. Displaying the alphabet this way, Head Start teachers can find opportunities to talk about individual letters with small groups or individual children.

As noted, preschoolers learn the alphabet when they realize it is important to **them.** And what is more meaningful to a preschooler than his or her name? High/Scope's *Letter Links: Alphabet Learning With Children's Names* (DeBruin-Parecki & Hohmann, 2003)

is a letter-learning system that pairs a child's printed nametag with a picture of something that starts with the same letter and sound (together, these are called a *letter link*). This is a way for children to learn the letters and letters sounds in their own names and the letters in their friends' names. Having the posted names of the children and their letter-linking pictures in your classroom will serve as meaningful environmental print and is more likely what the children will look at when they want to write something, rather than a store-bought alphabet poster. For example, Natasha wants to write her Mom a letter at work time. She knows that her classmate Morgan (who has the letter link *Motorcycle*) has an *M* in it because it sounds like *Mom*. Natasha goes to Morgan's nametag, copies her *M*, and starts her letter to her mother. Why wouldn't Natasha go to the posted alphabet train you ask? Because preschool children don't learn the alphabet

Letter Links and the Alphabetic Principle

How do letter links help preschool children figure out the alphabetic principle? Nametags and letter-linking pictures help preschool children to

- Identify the first letter in their name.

- Recognize that the first sound in their name and the first sound of the object pictured on their letter link are the same.

- Connect the first letter in their name to the sound it makes.

- Recognize that the letter *S* in *Sue* and the letter *s* in *sun*, for example, both make the /s/ sound.

- Learn the letter names and sounds of the first letters in classmates' names.

- Learn to recognize their own printed names and the printed names of some classmates.

- Begin to understand that their name is a word made up of an unvarying set of letters arranged in an unvarying order.

The Find-Use-Return Cycle

Arranging and labeling the learning environment so that children have easy access to materials helps establish the find-use-return cycle, which gives children experience with the key developmental indicator of classification while empowering them to select materials and participate in cleaning up.

Find:

Materials kept within easy sight and reach in this classroom make it possible for children to find what they want to use and then to join others in play.

Use:

These boys are using several of the different building materials they have chosen, finding more materials as needed to expand on their play idea.

Return:

At cleanup time, the children know right where to return the building materials they have used and enjoy the process of building with them once again!

in order; they learn and retain through active learning and by what is meaningful and important to them.

My Head Start classroom is very small, and most of my children like to go to the house area during work time. Is it okay in the High/Scope Curriculum to limit the number of children in that area at one time?

By limiting the number of children in an area, we may be communicating the message that their choices and plans are acceptable only some of the time. For example, if Tommie makes a plan to go to the house area and, when he gets there, he finds that it is now closed because other children who planned before him are now there, we are, in effect, saying that you can only make "some" choices or you can make a choice if you are quick about it in your planning. This policy does not respect children's choices and invalidates the planning process. Instead, consider that overcrowded areas and workspaces at work time are a problem to be solved.

First, look at your learning environment. If you have an area in your classroom that most of your children flock to at work time, think about what you can do to enlarge that area. Perhaps you can move a shelf to make more space available. Or maybe you arrange the area so that it flows freely into another area without the barrier of a piece of furniture — let your carpet or floor markings be how you define the areas. For example, many programs put the house area and block area next to one another so play can spill over into a larger space and children can easily transport materials from one area to another. Are there enough materials in that area that most of your children flock to? Having ample materials and multiple sets of materials is evidence of a high-quality classroom. Additionally, arranging the environ-

ment to help children establish the **find-use-return cycle** (see the illustration on p. 58) gives children greater access to *all* materials.

Second, honestly ask yourself, "Is this issue of too many children in one area **my** issue or the **children's** issue?" By observing how children play and interact in the area, the answer will become apparent. If there are no conflicts over space and materials, there is no problem to be solved. Children will naturally flow in and out of the area (and often children do not stay in the same area for the entire work time), and you can observe these movement patterns. If, on the other hand, crowding or a shortage of equipment and materials is causing conflicts, or you observe children approaching but backing away from the area in question, then consider involving them in solving the problem. Let's take a look at the following scenario.

Teacher: *Is everything okay over here? You seem a little frustrated. Are you getting everything you need here? Is there enough room to do your plan here?*

Child: *NO! I'm trying to make pizza in my restaurant and there are too many people in my way by the stove.*

Teacher: *There are too many people in your way? Oh … so the problem is that you want to cook pizza in your restaurant, but you can't seem to get to the stove. How can we solve this problem? Is there somewhere else in the room you can set up a restaurant to cook your pizza in?*

Child: (Looks around the room.) *Hey! There's nobody in the toy area.*

Teacher: *There sure isn't, and that looks like a cool place to set up a restaurant. Would you like me to help you move some things over? What will you need?*

After the teacher and child move items needed to set up restaurant, the teacher extends his play and learning as shown in the dialogue on the next page.

Teacher: *Let me know when your restaurant is open. I'm getting pretty hungry. Will you let me know when you put out your "open" sign so I can come make my order?*

Child: *Open sign? Oh, I need to make one. OK. Then I'll come get you when I'm ready.*

The teacher can now go back to the crowded area and see if any other children are uncomfortable.

Not only has this exchange between the teacher and child solved the problem, but the child has the satisfaction of having come up with an effective solution on his own. Don't hesitate to involve children in this process. Some Head Start programs hold a brief "class meeting" at greeting time or large-group time to address these types of space problems that affect everyone in the classroom. The children can be very creative problem solvers, and teachers may be surprised at what preschoolers can teach them!

Adult-Child Interactions

I am a Head Start center director. I don't feel comfortable allowing the students in my center to call the teachers by their first names. I feel that they won't learn to respect them if they don't say Miss or Mr. Some of my teaching staff feels the same way I do, and some don't mind at all. It is causing quite a disturbance at our center not only with the staff but also with the parents. What does High/Scope say about the use of children calling the adults in the classroom by their first names?

Feeling uncomfortable about the use of first names is not uncommon. Many people carry strong feelings from their childhoods when there were sometimes grave consequences if they, as children, called an adult by his or her first name. First, it is important to understand that children calling adults by their first name is not a requirement for you to run a High/Scope program — it is simply a matter of choice. As in all choices, you want to feel comfortable with the choices you make and their consequences.

The rationale behind why the children in many High/Scope classrooms call the adults by their first names stems from the adult-child interaction strategy of facilitating a *shared-control environment* in the classroom. We, the adults, are partners with the children in play and in conversation. We try our best to foster a community of learners; both adults and children learn from each other. We are not suggesting that there should be a laissez-faire attitude in the classroom, where the children run the classroom; nor are we promoting an authoritarian attitude, where the teachers make all the decisions and do not include the children or their interests and abilities in classroom activities. Instead, we recommend a shared-control partnership and treat each other (adults and children) accordingly.

Using everyone's first name is a way of showing friendship between adults and children. Whether I'm called Mrs. Rush or Kay in the classroom doesn't matter. What does matter is having a successful relationship with children and their parents. The key to successful relationships is fostering that mutual respect. Mutual respect goes both ways; the teachers receive much respect from the children because the teachers give much respect to the children. This is demonstrated by meeting the children where they are, accepting them for who they are, and also realizing their potential of who they can become. The children know that they are to listen to their teachers because their teachers listen to the children. They learn respect by being shown respect. They also know that the adults in the classroom are their teachers and are responsible for

High/Scope recommends a shared-control partnership between adults and children, in which both adults and children can learn from each other.

them and the classroom as well. But, most of all, they know that their teacher is their friend. To sum this up, consider the words of three-year-old Lute when asked, "What do you like about High/Scope?" during the 2007 Annual High/Scope International Conference. Without hesitation and with the biggest smile, he answered, "I love Sue!" (Sue is his teacher.)

I am a Head Start teacher and teach in the inner city where conditions are poor and poverty and crime are high. Most of the children in my care have very low self-esteem and a negative image of themselves. Because of this, how can High/Scope tell me that "praise" can hurt my children? Isn't that exactly what they need?

High/Scope is all about giving children what they need. So if the children you serve have low self-esteem and a negative image of themselves, your concern that they would need high self-esteem and a positive self-image is understandable. The question is how to do this most effectively. High/Scope demonstrates that using encouragement rather than praise helps to bolster children's self-esteem and self-image.

Many well-intentioned teachers have used praise to improve children's self-esteem and self-image, but the outcome can be just the opposite. Research from the field supports this conclusion. Alfie Kohn (1999), noted author of *Punished by Rewards: The Trouble With Gold Stars, Incentive Plans, A's, Praise, and Other Bribes,* explains the potential damage to children when adults use praise. Children learn to depend on adults for figuring out what is right or wrong, instead of developing this ability themselves. Rather than rely on their intrinsic motivation to learn, learning or "performing" is done in order to please others. Children lose the interest and ability to work and learn on their own. Since the educational system does not always supply external rewards (even well-intentioned teachers cannot praise every child every minute every day), children may not be motivated to become actively engaged in the learning process. By contrast, children who can evaluate their own performance with encouraging feedback from interested adults remain involved. Moreover, they are self-correcting; that is, they can ask questions of themselves and work to solve problems on their own. Learning is inherently satisfying. Furthermore, "praise" implies judgment. Preschoolers know that if you can judge them favorably, you can also judge them unfavorably. As a result, they may be afraid to take risks. Exploring or trying something new might result in "failure" from the adult's perspective, so children stick with what is safe and has earned them praise before.

Using encouraging comments can be much more beneficial to your Head Start children instead of empty praise statements like "Good job," "Great work," or "Pretty picture." To change those phrases into encouragement, you should make meaningful comments or ask meaningful questions. To do this, you should ask yourself, before commenting, *What about the job is good? What is it about the work that makes it great? What is in the picture that makes it pretty?* Asking yourself these questions will make your encouraging comments more realistic and meaningful to the child. For example, if 4-year-old SharR̀on, who is used to being praised comes to you and shows you her newly painted picture looking for your approval, think about focusing on the art, not the artist. Acknowledge her efforts and accomplishments by making genuine comments about her work. Ask her to describe her ideas and her process in making her picture. Focusing on her actions and what she is learning will let her know that you truly care about her and her self-esteem. It will also help her to build a more positive image of herself.

The teacher observing these children during work time will use their interest in Matchbox cars for a planning strategy.

Daily Routine

Can my planning strategy and my recall strategy be the same strategy on the same day?

It can, but because children are active learners, you will want to keep them actively involved in the strategies that you plan. Using the same activities may become boring to the child who really looks forward to learning new ways of doing things. Although children do need repetition, vary the strategies to keep it interesting and to meet the needs of different individuals. For example, for younger children, use a concrete planning strategy, such as having the children bring to the planning area one thing that they will work with or use during work time and say how they will use it. For older children, you may choose to use a more abstract strategy, such as having the children draw or write a story about what they did at work time during recall. If you are planning your strategies based on your children's interests and abilities, you should be able to come up with plenty of planning and recall strategies that are interesting to your particular group of children.

Remember to use props that include what you observed the children in your group using during work time. For example, if you observed a few children in your group using the Matchbox cars in the block area during work time, you may want to incorporate a planning strategy tomorrow where children can drive the Matchbox cars to an area on the map of the classroom of where they will work that day. Also think of your Domain Elements that you want to introduce. How can you turn those into a brief planning or recall strategy?

The purpose of recalling with children is to give them an opportunity to share their experiences, which helps them remember what they have done and see the result of following through on their plans. It is an important time not only for social interaction but also for cognitive development as well. Use your observations of children to learn more about how to plan strategies for them. Granted, there will be some favorite planning and recall strategies among your children that you will want to repeat sometimes, but just remember that variety **is** the spice of life. For more ideas on planning and recall strategies, see the Teacher's Idea Book *Making the Most of Plan-Do-Review* by Nancy Vogel (High/Scope Press, 2001).

Assessment

Speaking of observations, just how many anecdotes does High/Scope require I take on a preschool student?

To answer this question, keep in mind the reasons for taking anecdotes: to observe and plan each day for each child and the class as a whole, to complete the Preschool Child Observation Record (COR) for each child two to three times per year, to share developmental information about children with their parents, and to summarize and document student progress for administrative reporting purposes.

High/Scope does not put a number on how many anecdotes you need to take on a child. The "correct" number is whatever enables you and your program to meet the goals just stated. As a general rule, High/Scope advises teachers to make several observations per week per child. Sometimes Head Start agencies require a certain number of anecdotes. This policy may be instituted because of administrative concerns that teachers will wait until the last minute (e.g., just before it is time for a child's assessment or parent conferences) instead of making ongoing notes throughout the program year.

The best way to facilitate planning, serve children's developmental needs, and communicate with parents and administrators is to take regular notes on children. This does not mean one note for each child in each area every day. However, by looking back at your notes periodically, you can see where you need to fill in anecdotes on a particular child and/or area of development. Then you can be on the lookout for relevant examples.

As a guiding philosophy, consider the following encounter I had at a training session for camp counselors. A young lady found out I was an employee of the High/Scope Educational Research Foundation, and she said to me, "I really like the philosophy of High/Scope, but I don't like that assessment part where you just have to stand back and take a day to take notes on the kids. I'd rather be involved with them instead of observing them." I responded, "That's fantastic that you want to be involved with them, and I'm sure the children want you to be involved as well. I bet you would be able to take more in-depth and meaningful anecdotes on your children if you wrote them while you were involved and interacting with them." I suggested using sticky notes, a clipboard in each area, and other simple strategies for jotting things down. I also told her that she didn't need to write a complete anecdote on the spot — just enough to jog her memory so that at planning time she could fill in the details. "Try it and get back to me to let me know how it went," I concluded. At our next encounter she told me that she was able to get more out of her notes now that she has an easy way to do them that doesn't interrupt her playing and interacting with the children. She can now see much more growth developmentally, socially, and in all areas of their "bright little lives."

Appendix A: Steps to Implementing High/Scope

The following 10 steps will give you a concrete starting point for implementing High/Scope whether you are adapting it to an existing program or starting a new one.

1. Learn More About High/Scope
2. Identify Initial Implementation Goals
3. Establish a Timeline for Program Implementation
4. Address or Revisit Licensing Requirements
5. Develop a Staff Training Plan
6. Develop or Update Administrative Materials
7. Set Up the Learning Environment
8. Get the Word Out
9. Put High/Scope Into Practice!
10. Evaluate Your Program

❶ Learn More About High/Scope

Start on your High/Scope journey by doing a little research. Make sure the High/Scope Curriculum is a good fit for your program so that teachers will accept it and you will be able to adequately support them. You've already begun this step by picking up this book! Read other High/Scope publications or call the Foundation and talk to an early childhood teacher or specialist. Examine the photos and summary checklists in the books *Educating Young Children: Active Learning Practices for Preschool and Child Care Programs* (Hohmann, Weikart, & Epstein, 2008) and *Essentials of Active Learning in Preschool: Getting to Know the High/Scope Curriculum* (Epstein, 2007) to see if the High/Scope approach is right for your needs. You can also find a recommended list of publications for getting started with the High/Scope approach at the High/Scope online store. Contact High/Scope Press to request free informational brochures, a copy of High/Scope's *ReSource* magazine, or a catalog at

High/Scope Press
600 North River Street
Ypsilanti, MI 48198-2898
1-800-40-PRESS
www.highscope.org

After learning more about High/Scope, discuss the approach with your advisory board members and/or the owner/operator of your center to gain approval for moving forward with implementation. Share informational materials with each staff member to acquaint them with the High/Scope Foundation and the High/Scope Curriculum. Listen to staff ideas, opinions, and concerns, and answer their questions.

❷ Identify Initial Implementation Goals

Once the program staff members have decided to proceed with implementing the High/Scope Curriculum, meet with them as a whole group, as teaching teams, and individually to ensure their questions and needs are met both as individuals and as part of specific groups or teams.

Remember that change, even positive change, can be hard. Invite staff to see the challenge of adopting a new curriculum as an opportunity for professional growth. Some staff will be eager to begin and will want to implement High/Scope practices right away. Others will proceed with more caution and may wrestle with new practices and gain confidence gradually. And it is possible that others may resist the new practices altogether.

Encourage team members to take risks, and reassure them that you and the group will support their efforts. Be patient and accept even the smallest steps as success. Teachers and other classroom adults need to feel safe as they implement changes in the classroom and in their teaching styles. Encouraging staff to plan activities, carry them out, reflect on children's responses, and evaluate their own teaching behavior helps them become more insightful and leads to enduring curriculum change.

Choose one or two areas of the approach to begin with. Implementing High/Scope incrementally will allow you and your staff to proceed at a realistic pace.

Active participatory learning, child observation, and room arrangement are concrete starting points for teachers who are new to the approach. For example, you could begin by having teachers practice planning activities around child interests, practice making observations and taking notes on individual children's development, or practice arranging the room to foster children's play. These will be the areas and strategies you can focus on in your reading, training, and staff discussions. After staff have mastered these strategies, you can move onto other High/Scope components such as daily routines; adult-child interaction; children's learning in various content areas, such as reading, mathematics, conflict resolution, or art; assessments; family involvement; and team teaching and planning.

❸ Establish a Timeline for Program Implementation

As you prepare to implement High/Scope in your program, it will help to establish a timeline for completing the steps outlined in this guide. Additionally, determining your training needs will help you to establish a training calendar, which will help keep you on track to meeting your High/Scope implementation goals. You can use the reproducible implementation planning form found at the end of this appendix to set goals for meeting your objectives within each implementation step. Reviewing the following questions will also help you develop your timeline:

▼ When will you initiate implementation? Is one time of year more logical than another to transition to something new?

▼ How many classrooms will you have?

▼ How many staff members will be needed? (Tip: State licensing requirements will have a bearing on this — see Step 4.)

▼ Do you have a training budget to allow for training by a High/Scope certified trainer? (If not, see Step 5 for suggestions on other funding sources.)

▼ Are you pursuing a particular type of accreditation at the same time?

▼ What more do you need to learn about High/Scope's active participatory learning approach? Make a list and see the resources listed in Appendix B of this book or visit the High/Scope Web site at *www.highscope.org.*

▼ What are the backgrounds and philosophy of the teachers in your program? Do their backgrounds fit well with High/Scope's active learning approach?

▼ If you are an administrator, how much time do you have to dedicate to learning the material and assisting staff?

▼ Will there be other organizational changes in your program that are likely to affect curriculum implementation?

▼ How and where will you advertise your program?

▼ If your program operates year-round and all day, when will you be able to schedule training sessions?

▼ Do you know of another site that is implementing High/Scope that you can observe? If so, be sure to build time to do this into your implementation timeline. In addition, High/Scope maintains a list of High/Scope-accredited programs so you can find the closest one to your program to call on.

Your local child care resource and referral agency can also be of help during this step. Such agencies usually can provide helpful tips for getting started, sample forms, and information on licensing (which is also addressed in Step 4) and can put you in touch with other early childhood professionals for support and information sharing.

❹ Address or Revisit Licensing Requirements

Each state has its own requirements for licensing of early childhood centers. Among the issues covered in the licensing process are adult-to-child ratios, facilities, materials and equipment needed, health and safety requirements, and insurance matters. Contact your local child care resource and referral agency for guidance in the licensing process. Determine the steps you'll need to take and the amount of time the licensing process is likely to take so you can build these factors into your implementation timeline (e.g., you may be required to take safety, CPR, or first-aid classes). In the process, you are also likely to identify a number of resources that will come in handy during the program implementation process and beyond.

❺ Develop a Staff Training Plan

Training by High/Scope trainers. High/Scope offers a variety of training options ranging from one- to two-day workshops in child development and the High/Scope approach to multiple-week programs with options for certification as a High/Scope teacher or trainer. A limited amount of online training is also available and will increase in the future.

For more information on training options, setting up onsite training, or locating a training event taking place in your area, visit the High/Scope Web site at *www.highscope.org* or contact

Educational Services Department
Attention: Registration
600 North River Street
Ypsilanti, Michigan, 48198
734-485-2000, ext. 234
training@highscope.org

In-house training. It is very helpful to develop an in-house trainer. This person could be an administrator or a teacher in the classroom. Staff who serve as trainers are typically excited about the approach and are eager to serve as onsite experts and motivators! To supplement his or her hands-on experiences in the classroom, the in-house trainer can gain expertise by attending workshops given by High/Scope trainers, observing High/Scope classrooms in other High/Scope programs, and/or studying High/Scope books and videos.

When training others, focus on one thing at a time. Asking a teacher to change her classroom environment and her daily routine is unrealistic — too much information to absorb and implement at once. Make success achievable by breaking down large topics into manageable parts. For example, break training on the daily routine into a session on planning, a session on recalling, a session on work time, and so forth. Since many people learn best through concrete experiences, make sure training includes videos, observations in an actual classroom, and plenty of hands-on learning opportunities.

More experienced teachers who are comfortable with the High/Scope approach may be more easily able to implement new strategies after reading or discussing a new topic. These teachers can serve as mentors to less experienced teachers.

Keeping in mind that curriculum change takes time will allow you to invest resources in staff in such a way that changes will be long lasting.

Materials for staff study. In addition to the High/Scope reference books listed in Step 1 above, a few other books are worth listing here. The book series *Supporting Young Learners* addresses special topics, such as working with children with special needs and involving families in the early childhood program. The articles in this series are easy to read and balance theory and development with practical hints for the classroom. For ideas for classroom materials, see *Getting Started: Materials and Equipment for Active Learning Preschools* by Nancy Vogel (High/Scope Press, 1997). You will also find teaching strategies, classroom tips, and sample

activities in the many teacher idea books, music CDs, children's books, and parent flyers that are available for purchase through the High/Scope online store (*www.highscope.org*). See also Appendix B for additional High/Scope resources.

Because observing children is the first step in activity planning using the High/Scope approach, High/Scope offers a tool for observing and assessing children's development: the Preschool Child Observation Record (COR). The COR can be purchased in paper form or for use on the computer. The COR helps teachers record observations of child behavior, organize them under developmental areas, plan appropriate activities to further children's learning, and then assess children's growth. The COR can be used with both typically and nontypically developing infants, toddlers, and preschoolers. Learning to observe children is an important first step in planning activities around children's interests, so the COR is a good tool to use in the very first stages of implementing High/Scope. (See Appendix D for alignment of the COR with Head Start Indicators and the High/Scope Web site for information on COR training.)

Training budget. If the size of your budget is a concern, brainstorm ways to fund staff training and materials. For example, apply for grants from local resource and referral agencies or local businesses that support children's issues. Partner with other early childhood centers or organizations to split the training cost.

New staff. When interviewing job applicants, ask questions such as "How do you think children learn?" or "What is your philosophy of learning?" or "How would you teach a child the letters in the alphabet?" Applicants' answers won't include all the language used in High/Scope materials but will help you think about their ability to implement the High/Scope approach with its focus on active learning and sharing control with children.

Start High/Scope training right away for new employees. Provide, at minimum, training on the principles of active learning — preferably before they even enter the classroom. If possible, give new staff time to observe in another High/Scope classroom where the teaching staff are excited about what they are doing!

Provide journals so that new employees can keep a record of their comments, questions, and feelings about what they are learning. Take the time with new staff to read and discuss their journal entries periodically.

❻ Develop or Update Administrative Materials

Before you can finalize the details of your program and begin enrolling children, there are several administrative tasks to attend to that will help your program run smoothly. The results will help you convey your mission and philosophy to the families who enroll in your program, which is a key to your success!

Information Materials

If you are starting a new program, you will need to develop policies, forms, and parent handouts or a parent handbook. Your local child care resource and referral agency can help you with this and may even be able to provide templates of forms you need. Below you will also find a list of areas in which you may need to develop policies and written materials. If you are adapting an existing program, you may need to change or update some of your policies and forms. Also, be sure to inform parents and others about changes in your curriculum and approach. This can be part of your communication management plan.

Topics to address in program policies:

▼ Curriculum information (what curriculum is used, accreditation/appropriate practices information)

▼ Hours of operation

▼ Philosophy and mission statement

▼ Enrollment eligibility (What age group is served? Is state reimbursement accepted for lower income/special needs?)

▼ Immunization requirements

▼ Parent involvement opportunities

▼ Special offerings (Are computers available? Are any teachers bilingual? Will other special services or unique features be offered?)

▼ Technology policy (Are computers, digital cameras, cell phones, and e-mails to parents used? If so, in what ways, and how often?)

▼ Child abuse policy and reporting information

▼ The center's licensing organization

▼ Daily check-in and check-out procedures

▼ Fire evacuation procedures

▼ Meals and snacks (For instance, will you follow USDA or Child and Adult Care Food Program [CACFP] requirements in providing these?)

▼ Behavioral guidance policy (e.g., include information on taking a proactive approach, having age-appropriate expectations, having plentiful materials for children, using consistency in routines, using "I" statements to own feelings, and using the six steps to conflict resolution)

Frequently used forms:

▼ Accident report

▼ Illness report

▼ Field trip permission

▼ Information forms to create a file for each child that includes the following information, at minimum:

  – Emergency contacts/authorized pickup

  – Parent contact information

  – Photo release

- Immunization record
- Personal history (name, likes/dislikes, personality traits, and so forth)
- Allergies/health issues (Does the child have food allergies? Does the child require medications?)

▼ Lesson plan form: Each program will develop its own lesson plan form, based on its daily routine components. In other words, you do not have to purchase any planning forms or documents on an ongoing basis from the High/Scope Foundation. Since each program has its own special planning requirements, any format that covers the minimum daily routine components meets High/Scope planning guidelines. See the sample lesson plan forms used by the High/Scope Demonstration Preschool and two Head Start programs at the end of this appendix.

A Communication Plan

Parents play a vital role in every program, and particularly in Head Start programs, where parents are involved in all levels of Head Start policy and decision making from the classroom to the center to the city, state, and national level. Determine with other staff members the policy for communicating regularly with parents. As a team, discuss issues related to face-to-face discussions during arrival and departure times, using phone calls and e-mail messages to keep busy parents updated on significant events or to ask a parent a question, and communicating in other forms. See Chapter 2 for more on communication strategies.

Keep parents informed and educated about *any* changes that might take place in your program. Here are some strategies:

▼ Distribute parent handbooks and brochures that introduce the High/Scope Curriculum to parents, so they are aware of what their child's learning experiences will be.

▼ Send home newsletters that detail upcoming changes.

▼ Schedule regular parent meetings so that parents are able to hear about High/Scope and ask questions about how the curriculum changes being implemented in your program will affect their child.

▼ Offer workshops for parents to learn about the curriculum and how it supports learning opportunities in the home.

▼ Invite parents to observe the program and schedule a follow-up meeting or phone call to answer their questions.

Staff Schedules

Consistency is the key when scheduling staff. Strive for having the same staff in your program every day. Substitutes should be consistent as well so that the children experience as few changes in their lives as possible. Make sure you have enough adults on hand to meet requirements for adult-child ratios and to be able to safely and effectively carry out activities.

If there are several teachers in your program, strive to create teaching teams that balance or complement team members' skills. Take into consideration teachers' past experiences and their personal strengths in various curriculum areas. Also keep in mind differences in individual styles. For example, some classroom adults are very creative and spontaneous, and they can tolerate higher noise levels. Other adults may need more structure and order. Children also relate differently to adults with different styles, so it is a good idea to offer children variety. Strive to create teams that will work well together and enhance every area of the classroom.

Also make sure that schedules overlap for team planning time. Daily planning is the goal, but due to bus schedules, payroll issues, and other factors, sometimes team members can only meet every few days or weekly. It is important to meet as frequently as possible to plan activities that meet the rapidly changing skills of young children. In the beginning, classroom adults may require some time to get used to daily planning. However, once teams become proficient in planning, 15–20 minutes is usually enough time to record observations, compare notes, and plan for the next day. See Chapter 3 for sample daily routines that include team planning.

If you are the only teacher in a small program, be sure to take time each day to plan activities for the next day based on what you observe about children's interests and play ideas.

❼ Set Up the Learning Environment

There are many Head Start programs that use High/Scope successfully in a variety of physical settings. Keeping health and safety guidelines in mind, use what you have learned about creating child-centered, active learning environments to set up the activity areas in your own classroom. Know that you will adapt the learning areas over time in response to children's needs and interests. Also keep in mind that it is important to make the space comfortable for adults as well, since this will lend to children's sense of comfort and security.

Acquiring materials for children. High/Scope is not an expensive approach to implement — costly toys and materials are not required! You will likely need to make some purchases, however, in order to have sufficient variety and quantity of materials. (For more on selecting materials, see *Educating Young Children* by Mary Hohmann, David Weikart, and Ann Epstein [High/Scope Press, 2008] and *Essentials of Active Learning in Preschool* by Ann Epstein [High/Scope Press, 2007].) But remember that such open-ended materials as teacher-made items, natural materials, and donated household articles or personal items (e.g., old watches or purses) work well in the active

learning environment. Tap parents and local resources to build a stock of materials that reflect the diversity and uniqueness of the families you work with. Always be aware of toy and material safety issues for whatever you add to your classroom.

❽ Get the Word Out

Now that you have your policies and information forms in place and your program setting is arranged for active learning, it is time to let families know about your program! Here are some ways that you can get the word out:

▼ Make sure your local resource and referral agency has you listed in its database/directory.

▼ If your budget permits, advertise in a local parenting newspaper or magazine.

▼ Network with other center directors, and let them know that if they are full to capacity they may refer families to you.

▼ Leave flyers in places that families and children frequent, such as recreation centers, story-hour areas at book stores, grocery stores, and toy stores.

▼ Make connections in the community (e.g., at church functions, play groups, parks, and story hour at the public library).

▼ Hold an open house.

Perhaps the best advertising strategy is simply word of mouth. New families will undoubtedly talk with other friends and family members. They will share whether they think the center is worthwhile.

❾ Put High/Scope Into Practice!

As you begin using the High/Scope approach with the children enrolled in your program, reflect on the new techniques, teaching strategies, and styles of interaction that staff are using in each area of the approach. Keeping a journal of thoughts and experiences can help staff members self-reflect and generate topics for discussion with other staff during planning meetings and at other times.

Refining schedules. Once your program is up and running, you may find it necessary to reevaluate staffing schedules. Here are some things to keep in mind:

▼ As the program builds and your enrollment increases, you will need additional staff. Plan ahead by advertising for upcoming positions.

▼ According to the recent reauthorization of Head Start, by 2011 all Head Start teachers should have at least an associate's degree and 50 percent should have a bachelor's degree (Center for Law and Social Policy, n.d.). Note that this will affect how staff are to be placed your program.

▼ Remember that you must maintain proper adult-to-child ratios.

▼ Staff have personal lives that may require that they change or slightly alter their schedules. Try to be responsive to their needs. For example, someone may be attending a local college at night to earn a bachelor's degree. Perhaps for one semester he or she must leave 15 minutes earlier than scheduled to get to class. Can another person on staff provide the extra coverage? Can the teacher's schedule be switched with someone else's? Will the ratios allow the teacher to leave early?

▼ Remaining flexible and responsive will keep the team cohesive and well functioning, which means classroom adults will be able to thoughtfully observe and support children and make lesson plans built on children's interests.

⑩ Evaluate Your Program

Head Start programs must use the PRISM (Program Review Instrument for Systems Monitoring) assessment tool every three years. Each agency should complete a self-assessment for the city or grantee level, which, in turn, prepares the agency for the regional and federal review.

You can also use High/Scope's program evaluation tool, the Program Quality Assessment (PQA), before (as well as during and after) implementation of High/Scope at your site. Once you begin implementing High/Scope, using the PQA will help you evaluate your program for quality implementation and continuous improvement. The PQA can help you identify areas for further development and training, and provides concrete examples for participants to use in creating an implementation action plan. (For more information on the PQA and ways it can be used in implementing High/Scope, improving your program, and meeting accountability standards, see Appendix D and the High/Scope Web site.)

Start assessing teachers with the PQA tool when they have been working with the High/Scope approach for quite a while. Beginners will always rate lower on the scale of implementation, and low scores can lead to low morale and feelings of inefficacy. Just as the High/Scope approach respects children's individual development, it takes into account the individual pace of teachers' professional growth and development. Deciding when to use the PQA to evaluate a teacher should be a team decision between the teacher, the program director, and/or the person who will perform the PQA evaluation.

When using the PQA to evaluate teachers, use only sections in which they have received training and had time to implement changes. Focus on one area of growth rather than trying to complete an entire PQA, which can be overwhelming for both the observer and the classroom teachers.

Enjoy the Journey!

The High/Scope approach uses the same philosophy to support both classroom adults and children. Adults actively learn about their children's growth and development and bring their own interests and abilities to the teaching team. Collaborating in this way with peers, parents, and community partners helps to continuously improve the program. Therefore, as you implement High/Scope, remember that the quality of the process is also important to your goals. Enjoying the journey will ultimately help children learn and grow!

The following pages provide sample forms that you may use as models as you implement your new program. Completed planning sheets are also included so that you can see how other programs use their center-specific forms.

Sample Implementation Planning Form

(*Note:* You can use the blank implementation planning form on the next page to develop your own plans.)

Today's Date: January 2, 2008

Implementation Step: Step 7, Set up the Learning Environment

Goal: Have environmental changes in place within six months

Target date for goal achievement: June 30

Training needed: Learning Environment two-day workshop

Best training days: First or last week in March

Other resources needed for training: Learning Environment video and *Getting Started* books for each classroom

Staff needed to implement the change: All staff

Actions needed:

1. Call High/Scope Foundation to schedule training workshop.

2. Schedule coverage for one person from each room to attend training workshops.

3. Schedule in-house training with part-time afternoon employees.

4. Order *Learning Environment* video and *Getting Started* books for each classroom.

5. Distribute teacher wish list for new classroom materials.

6. Compile wish lists and place order to toy/furniture companies by May 1.

Follow-up steps:

- Schedule dates with each teaching team for evaluation with the Program Quality Assessment: June 15.

- Determine whether the goal was successfully met. If it was not, discuss reasons and set a new goal to achieve success.

- New target implementation date: January 16, 2008

- Target date for next evaluation: January 23, 2008

Implementation Planning Form

Today's Date: _____

Implementation Step: _____

Goal: _____

Target date for goal achievement: _____

Training needed: _____

Best training days: _____

Other resources needed for training: _____

Staff needed to implement the change: _____

Actions needed:

1. _____

2. _____

3. _____

4. _____

5. _____

6. _____

Follow-up steps:

- Schedule dates for PQA.

- Determine whether the goal was successfully met. If it was not, discuss reasons and set a new goal to achieve success.

- New target implementation date: _____

- Target date for next evaluation: _____

Sample Demonstration Preschool Daily Plan

Date: May 9, 2007	Adults: Sue and Shannon
Greeting Time: Read books* Door: Sue Books: Shannon	Child Messages:* Kay's birthday — cupcakes at snack New material in toy area — snap beads Song book — Naptyla
Shannon's Group	**Sue's Group**
Planning Time:* Toss the letter beanbags in the buckets with area signs of where you will work today (PD).	Use a planning sheet maze — follow the path to the area you will work in using colored pencils (M).
Work Time: Support children in block area. Look out for sorting for anecdotes. Encourage children to clean as you go (put toys away if finished before going to another area).	
Cleanup: 5 min. warning — ring bells — give out cleanup tickets with numbers. Children put away corresponding # of materials and receive another ticket.	
Recall Time:* Small, medium, and large paper bags. Children choose which size bag they'll need to put something in they played with.	Writing a recall story — each child draws or writes his own page, to make one big storybook.
Snack/Story:* Alphabet pretzels, Kay's cupcakes, milk Tommie's choice of storybook (Shannon's group), Marion's choice of storybook (Sue's group)	
Large-Group Time: Easy-to-join — Follow, follow, follow _____ Song book Fruit basket upset (when you hear the magic fruit, get up and change seats, find another space).	
Small-Group Time: Play dough and letter and number cookie cutters. Backup materials: Rolling pins and plastic knives	Mixing paints — Use blue and red paint only. Children will use paints/mix paints. Paint brushes, paper, and water. Backup materials: White and black paint to add for tints.
Outside Time: Take out bikes, sandbox toys, Hula-Hoops, balls, and jump ropes.	
To Remember: Distribute permission slips to parents.	Parent Messages: Remember field trip to the zoo (5/25).

*Denotes Literacy Activity

Key Developmental Indicators (KDIs)
AL Approaches to Learning   **LL** Language, Literacy, & Communication   **SE** Social & Emotional Development   **PD** Physical Development, Health, & Well-Being

Sample of Small-Group-Time Planning Sheet

Originating idea: Toothbrush Mural — After the toothbrushes became frayed and it was time to get new ones for tooth brushing, some of the children asked, "What happened to the old ones?"

Materials:
✔ Old, used discarded toothbrushes that have been sanitized

✔ A long sheet of roll paper (make sure it is wide enough so children seated on both sides will have room to paint but narrow enough so that they can easily reach the middle of the paper)

✔ Muffin tins to hold paint and water or small cups

✔ For backup materials: Cotton swabs or cotton balls

Possible key developmental indicators:
Social and Emotional Development: Creating and experiencing collaborative play

Science and Technology — Classification: Using and describing something in several ways

Science and Technology — Classification: Exploring and describing similarities, differences, and the attributes of things

The Arts — Visual Art: Drawing and painting

Beginning (with opening statement): Gather children around the long piece of paper on the floor or a long table. Remind them that they just received brand new toothbrushes today: "Today, instead of using your old toothbrushes for brushing your teeth, you can use them to paint designs on the paper."
Give each child his or her own set of materials — toothbrush, paint, and water

Middle: Watch and observe the ways children paint; be supportive of the different ways they use the paint. Recognize each child's individual effort. Use strategies that support children based on their actions. Notice ways children interact with each other when they want more colors or to switch colors. Help children who need assistance in expressing their needs.

End: Give a 5-minute warning that small-group time will end; bring a tub of soapy water to the table for cleanup. Ask children to wash their toothbrushes and paint containers and store them in the art area, in the new, labeled container for the toothbrushes. Engage children in find a suitable drying spot for the mural.

Follow-up: Hang the mural in the bathroom or other area where children brush their teeth in your center. Remind children that the old toothbrushes are stored in the art area and are available to use during work time.

Adapted from Michelle Graves, *Explore and Learn Quick Cards: 80 Activities for Small Groups* (Ypsilanti, MI: High/Scope Press, 2007).

Sample of Large-Group-Time Planning Sheet

Originating idea: Little Miss Muffet — Teachers and children have been reading Mother Goose nursery rhymes during greeting and reading times. Children have been noticing words that rhyme with their names. Teachers are looking for an active way to further support the understanding of the meaning of rhymes.

Materials:
✔ A large pillow

✔ A bowl and a spoon

✔ Two large nametags labeled "Miss Muffet" and "Spider" (made of paper or cardboard hung on a string to go around child's neck)

✔ A piece of chart paper with the rhyme "Little Miss Muffet" written on it

Possible key developmental indicators:
The Arts — Dramatic Art: Pretending and role playing
Language, Literacy, and Communication — Having fun with language: listening to stories and poems, making up stories and rhymes
Approaches to Learning — Making and expressing choices, plans, and decisions

Beginning (with opening statement): Post the chart paper with the words to Little Miss Muffet where all can see it. Ask children to listen for rhyming words while they say it together with you. Then ask them to tell you the rhyming words they heard. Discuss the meaning of "tuffet" and "curds and whey": something you sit on (small stool or pillow) and cottage cheese (curds are the lumps and whey is the liquid). Explain to the children that they will be acting out the nursery rhyme Little Miss Muffett and that each child that wants to can play the roles of Little Miss Muffet and the spider.

Middle: Place the pillow in the middle of the large-group space to serve as a tuffet. Choose two children to wear the signs and play the roles as the children and teachers recite the rhyme together. Children may choose to perform another action as Miss Muffet instead of run away. Ask children to change the spider to another animal of their choice. Ask children to give suggestions for new animals and new movements. Ask children to change the /m/ sound in Miss Muffet to the initial sound of the child who is playing Miss Muffet (e.g., if Karla is on the pillow, they would say "Little Kiss Kuffet").

End: After several children have taken turns as Miss Muffet and the spider, dismiss the children from large group to the next part of the daily routine by using their names two or three at a time in a variation of the rhyme (e.g., "Mary and Charles sat on a tuffet" — when children hear their names they leave the group).

Follow-up: Keep the nametags in the classroom so children can reenact the rhyme during work time. Use the rhyme to transition children in and out of activities during other times of the day.

Adapted from Christine Boisvert and Suzanne Gainsley, *Explore and Learn Quick Cards: 50 Activities for Large Groups* (Ypsilanti, MI: High/Scope Press, 2008).

Sample Head Start Weekly Lesson Plan*

Delegate: __TOFM__

Center: __Home of Love__

Teaching Team: Havard, Tutt; Alston, Qualls; Graves, Kirksey

Week of: __10-22-07__

Head Start Outcomes Goal:

1. Creative Representation

2. Language

Activities	Monday	Tuesday	Wednesday	Thursday	Friday		
Large Group	Song book If Your Name Starts With (STEP activity)	Song book Yoga exercise	Song book "Pizza Pizza"	Song book "Sticky Icky Bubble Gum" Yoga exercise			
Planning Time	Fish for your first name and plan (STEP activity)	Children will bring back something they will work with.	Children will choose their favorite fruit and place it in the area they will work in.	Children will string a bead for each plan that they make.			
Recall Time	Fish for your last name and recall (STEP activity)	Number ring toss — Children will first recall and then toss the number of rings according to the number of areas they played in, number of things they played with, etc.	Write children's name on bottom of plastic food. Put food in bag. Each child pulls out a piece of food, and indentifies the food and the child's name whose turn it is to recall.	Children will identify the shapes and tell what they did in that area.			
Language	Message board "read" by child	See Planning Time	Helper chart "read" by child	Message board "read" by child			
Literacy	See Planning Time and Large Group Author's Chair	Author's Chair	Chicka Chicka Boom Boom Sit	Author's Chair			

*Every City of Detroit Head Start is required to complete a weekly lesson plan. Because the Home of Love Center follows the High/Scope Curriculum, the teachers plan daily and use a daily sheet plan (see p. 82).

(Continued on next page)

Sample Head Start Weekly Lesson Plan

Activities	Monday	Tuesday	Wednesday	Thursday	Friday
Creative Art	See Small Group	See Large Group — Yoga	See Small Group	See Small Group and Large Group — Yoga	
Math	See Gross Motor	See Recall Time	See Language: Sorting out who at what table has what job	See Planning time; see Wed.	
Science	Children will add colors to shaving cream	Children will explore shakers	See Nutrition	See Small Group Painting	
Dramatic Play	Menus to place orders added to the house area	Have new clothes — added African dress	Explore added dress-up clothes	Doctor, vet prop box added to house area	
Computers	Let's Create a Word Program	JumpStart Program	Let's Create a Word Program	JumpStart Program	
Parent Input	Autumn leaves. Children will describe leaves on tree.				
Gross Motor *Indoor/Outdoor*	Children will hunt for numbers on walk to and from the playground.	Children will hunt for letters on walk to and from the playground.	Children will look for shapes on walk to and from the playground.	Children will read symbols on walk (e.g., M for McDonald's, sign for stop sign, etc.).	
Adaptation	N/A	N/A	N/A	N/A	

(Continued on next page)

Sample Head Start Weekly Lesson Plan

Activities	Monday	Tuesday	Wednesday	Thursday	Friday
Nutrition Dental Health & Safety Mental Health	Health materials available in book area — Cough and sneeze book "If you cough and sneeze, cover your mouth please"	Mental health — see Planning Time	Nutrition and Dental — Fruit feast; creating a fruit parfait; see Planning Time also	See Wed.	
Small Group	Children will explore with shaving cream	Children will explore floor puzzles	Children will create a fruit collage	Children will explore with paint and Q-tips	
Children's Special Interests					

Special Event:

Parent Curriculum Input: J Powers

Center Manager's Signature: Lorraine Havard

*Thirty minutes of Language and Literacy per day

*Transition activity once a month

*Nutrition activity should be once a week (food preparation once a month)

*Dental, Health & Safety, or Mental Health activity once a week

Source: Adapted from The Order of the Fishermen Ministry Head Start Home of Love Center, Detroit, MI.

Sample Head Start Daily Lesson Plan

A.M. & P.M.	
Adults Graves Kirksey	**Date:** 1-2-08
Greeting Time Door Graves Books Kirksey	**Child Messages:** Job assignments Who's absent? New books for Black History Month
Planning Time Graves — String beads while making plans (# of beads = # of plans) Kirksey — Children will pick a number from a bag, identify it, and make that number of plans	
Work Time Support children solving problems with materials Look for children using and comparing properties (anecdotes)	
Clean-up 5-minute warning from cleanup captain; sing "Put Away Song"	
Recall Time Graves — Children draw with chalk and boards what they did at work time Kirksey — Recall train: Each child leads the train to the area he or she worked in	
Large-Group Time Song book choices from children Using streamers to fast and slow music	
Small-Group Time Graves — Shaving cream art Kirksey — Read the story "Chicka Chicka Boom Boom," and then cut letters from magazines and glue on trees	
Outside Time Balls, shovels for snow, buckets to collect snow Playground equipment	
To Remember	**Parent Message** Remind parents of Black History Celebration 2/28

Source: Adapted from The Order of the Fishermen Ministry Head Start Home of Love Center, Detroit, Michigan.

Sample Head Start Daily Lesson Plan

Classroom/Session Neiman/Carroll		Date: 1-2-08 Mon. Tues. (Wed.) Thurs. Fri.		
Greeting Time: Greet all who enter Sign in Choose jobs for today		**Child Messages:** Who's absent?		

	IEP/ILP	LA	SA
Large Group: Good morning song (Eng/Spanish) Movement exercise — Children choose song and exercises for the routine.			
Small Group 1: Journaling — Children draw pictures in their journals and talk to teacher about it. The teacher writes and reads what they say about it.		✔	
Small Group 2: Making books — After reading the story "Froggy Loves Books," children use book-making materials to make their own book.		✔	
Planning 1: Spin the bottle — wherever it stops, make your plan.			
Planning 2: Using scissors, cut out the area that they will work in today from planning sheet.			
Work Time: Teacher 1 — Support children in block area **Teacher 2** — Encourage children and remind about works in progress			
Cleanup Time: 5-min. hand; cleanup hand Cots Bathroom			
Recall — Group 1: Bring something to the table you worked with at work time and trace it.			
Recall — Group 2: Flashlights — Children will shine the light on the area they worked in while talking about it.			
Gross Motor Activity: Outside — Use balls, scooters, swings, and slides.			
Things to Remember: Support children being toilet trained by reminding.			

LA = Literacy Activity   SA = Service-Area Activity

Source: Adapted from Adrian Head Start Comstock Center, Adrian, Michigan.

Appendix B: Guide to High/Scope Resources

You can find more information on topics discussed in this book through the following resources.

High/Scope Active Learning Approach

For a detailed description of the High/Scope approach, see

▼ *Educating Young Children: Active Learning Practices for Preschool and Child Care Programs* by Mary Hohmann, David P. Weikart, and Ann S. Epstein (High/Scope Press, 2008)

▼ *Essentials of Active Learning in Preschool: Getting to Know the High/Scope Curriculum* by Ann S. Epstein (High/Scope Press, 2007)

You can also find a wealth of information on the High/Scope approach, High/Scope materials, and High/Scope training at the High/Scope Web site (*www.highscope.org*).

Daily Routine

For descriptions and activities for specific parts of the daily routine, see

▼ *The Daily Routine* (video and DVD)

▼ *High/Scope Step by Step: Lesson Plans for the First 30 Days* by Beth Marshall (High/Scope Press, 2007)

▼ *Making the Most of Plan-Do-Review* (Teacher's Idea Book Series) by Nancy Vogel (High/Scope Press, 2001)

▼ *Planning Around Children's Interests* (Teacher's Idea Book Series) by Michelle Graves (High/Scope Press, 1996)

▼ *Explore and Learn Quick Cards: 80 Activities for Small Groups* by Michelle Graves (High/Scope Press, 2007)

▼ *Explore and Learn Quick Cards: 50 Activities for Large Groups* by Christine Boisvert and Suzanne Gainsley (High/Scope Press, 2008)

▼ *50 Large-Group Activities for Active Learners* (Teacher's Idea Book Series) by Christine Boisvert and Suzanne Gainsley (High/Scope Press, 2006)

▼ *Large-Group Times for Active Learners* (video and DVD)

▼ *Small-Group Times for Active Learners* (video and DVD)

▼ *"I Know What's Next!" Preschool Transitions Without Tears or Turmoil* by Betsy Evans (High/Scope Press, 2007)

▼ *Let's Go Outside! Designing the Early Childhood Playground* by Tracy Theemes (High/Scope Press, 1999)

Literacy Tools

▼ Growing Readers Early Literacy Curriculum (GRC) (High/Scope Press, 2005)

▼ Growing Readers Early Literacy Curriculum: Set 2 (High/Scope Press, 2008)

▼ *Storybook Talk: Conversations for Comprehension* by Mary Hohmann and Kate Adams (High/Scope Press, 2008)

▼ *From Message to Meaning: Using a Daily Message Board in the Preschool Classroom* by Suzanne Gainsley (High/Scope Press, 2008)

▼ *Let's Talk Literacy: Practical Readings for Preschool Teachers* edited by Mary Hohmann and Joanne Tangorra (High/Scope Press, 2007)

▼ *Letter Links: Alphabet Learning With Children's Names* by Andrea DeBruin-Parecki and Mary Hohmann (High/Scope Press, 2003) [Spanish version available]

▼ *Fee, Fie, Phonemic Awareness: 130 Pre-reading Activities for Preschoolers* by Mary Hohmann (High/Scope Press, 2002)

▼ *Preschool Readers and Writers: Early Literacy Strategies for Teachers* by Linda Ranweiler (High/Scope Press, 2004)

▼ Early Literacy Skills Assessment (ELSA) (High/Scope Press, 2004)

Child Observation and Assessment; Communicating With Parents

For strategies that support observation, assessment, and communicating with parents, see

▼ *The Essential Parent Workshop Resource* by Michelle Graves (High/Scope Press, 2000)

▼ *Educating Young Children* by Mary Hohmann, David P. Weikart, and Ann S. Epstein (High/Scope Press, 2008)

▼ *Essentials of Active Learning in Preschool* by Ann S. Epstein (High/Scope Press, 2007)

For child observation and assessment, see

▼ Child Observation Record (COR), Second Edition (High/Scope Press, 2003)

Conflict Resolution

For strategies and examples of conflict resolution, see

▼ *You Can't Come to My Birthday Party! Conflict Resolution With Young Children* by Betsy Evans (High/Scope Press, 2002)

▼ *Educating Young Children* by Mary Hohmann, David P. Weikart, and Ann S. Epstein (High/Scope Press, 2008)

▼ *Essentials of Active Learning in Preschool* by Ann S. Epstein (High/Scope Press, 2007)

▼ *Supporting Children in Resolving Conflicts* (video and DVD)

▼ *It's Mine! Responding to Problems and Conflicts* (video and DVD)

Find-Use-Return Cycle

For ways to implement the find-use-return cycle, see

▼ *Educating Young Children* by Mary Hohmann, David P. Weikart, and Ann S. Epstein (High/Scope Press, 2008)

▼ *Essentials of Active Learning in Preschool* by Ann S. Epstein (High/Scope Press, 2007)

Children With Special Needs

For using the High/Scope Curriculum with children with special needs, see

▼ *I Belong: Active Learning for Children With Special Needs* by Jan Levanger Dowling and Terri C. Mitchell (High/Scope Press, 2007)

▼ *High/Scope for Children With Special Needs: A Developmental Approach* (video and DVD)

Designing Environments/ Labeling

For practical advice on designing environments and making child-friendly labeling, see

▼ *Educating Young Children* by Mary Hohmann, David P. Weikart, and Ann S. Epstein (High/Scope Press, 2008)

▼ *Essentials of Active Learning in Preschool* by Ann S. Epstein (High/Scope Press, 2007)

Safety

You can find guidelines on toy safety at the Web site for the U.S. Consumer Product Safety Commission at *www.cpsc.gov/cpscpub/pubs/281.pdf*

Program Assessment

▼ Preschool Program Quality Assessment (PQA), Second Edition (High/Scope Press, 2003)

Mathematics

For more information on mathematic activities, see

▼ *"I'm Older Than You. I'm Five!" Math in the Preschool Classroom* by Ann S. Epstein and Suzanne Gainsley (High/Scope Press, 2005)

The Arts

For more information on the arts, see

▼ *Supporting Young Artists: The Development of the Visual Arts in Young Children* by Ann S. Epstein and Eli Trimis (High/Scope Press, 2002)

Appendix C: Head Start Child Outcomes Framework

Domain	Domain Element	Indicators
Language Development	Listening & Understanding	◆ Demonstrates increasing ability to attend to and understand conversations, stories, songs, and poems. ◆ Shows progress in understanding and following simple and multiple-step directions. ★ Understands an increasingly complex and varied vocabulary. ★ For non-English-speaking children, progresses in listening to and understanding English.
	Speaking & Communicating	★ Develops increasing abilities to understand and use language to communicate information, experiences, ideas, feelings, opinions, needs, questions; and for other varied purposes. ◆ Progresses in abilities to initiate and respond appropriately in conversation and discussions with peers and adults. ★ Uses an increasingly complex and varied spoken vocabulary. ◆ Progresses in clarity of pronunciation and towards speaking in sentences of increasing length and grammatical complexity. ★ For non-English-speaking children, progresses in speaking English.

★ *Indicates the four specific Domain Elements and nine Indicators that are legislatively mandated.*

Source: U.S. Department of Health and Human Services (2003).

Domain	Domain Element	Indicators
Literacy	★ Phonological Awareness	◆ Shows increasing ability to discriminate and identify sounds in spoken language. ◆ Shows growing awareness of beginning and ending sounds of words. ◆ Progresses in recognizing matching sounds and rhymes in familiar words, games, songs, stories, and poems. ◆ Shows growing ability to hear and discriminate separate syllables in words. ★ **Associates sounds with written words,** such as awareness that different words begin with the same sound.
	★ Book Knowledge & Appreciation	◆ Shows growing interest and involvement in listening to and discussing a variety of fiction and non-fiction books and poetry. ◆ Shows growing interest in reading-related activities, such as asking to have a favorite book read; choosing to look at books; drawing pictures based on stories; asking to take books home; going to the library; and engaging in pretend-reading with other children. ◆ Demonstrates progress in abilities to retell and dictate stories from books and experiences; to act out stories in dramatic play; and to predict what will happen next in a story. ◆ Progresses in learning how to handle and care for books; knowing to view one page at a time in sequence from front to back; and understanding that a book has a title, author, and illustrator.
	★ Print Awareness & Concepts	◆ Shows increasing awareness of print in classroom, home, and community settings. ◆ Develops growing understanding of the different functions of forms of print such as signs, letters, newspapers, lists, messages, and menus. ◆ Demonstrates increasing awareness of concepts of print, such as that reading in English moves from top to bottom and from left to right, that speech can be written down, and that print conveys a message. ◆ Shows progress in recognizing the association between spoken and written words by following print as it is read aloud. ★ **Recognizes a word as a unit of print,** or awareness that letters are grouped to form words, and that words are separated by spaces.

★ *Indicates the four specific Domain Elements and nine Indicators that are legislatively mandated.*

Domain	Domain Element	Indicators
Literacy	Early Writing	◆ Develops understanding that writing is a way of communicating for a variety of purposes. ◆ Begins to represent stories and experiences through pictures, dictation, and in play. ◆ Experiments with a growing variety of writing tools and materials, such as pencils, crayons, and computers. ◆ Progresses from using scribbles, shapes, or pictures to represent ideas, to using letter-like symbols, to copying or writing familiar words such as their own name.
	Alphabet Knowledge	◆ Shows progress in associating the names of letters with their shapes and sounds. ◆ Increases in ability to notice the beginning letters in familiar words. ★ Identifies at least 10 letters of the alphabet, especially those in their own name. ★ Knows that letters of the alphabet are a special category of visual graphics that can be individually named.
Mathmatics	★ Number & Operations	◆ Demonstrates increasing interest and awareness of numbers and counting as a means for solving problems and determining quantity. ◆ Begins to associate number concepts, vocabulary, quantities, and written numerals in meaningful ways. ◆ Develops increasing ability to count in sequence to 10 and beyond. ◆ Begins to make use of one-to-one correspondence in counting objects and matching groups of objects. ◆ Begins to use language to compare numbers of objects with terms such as more, less, greater than, fewer, equal to. ◆ Develops increased abilities to combine, separate, and name "how many" concrete objects.

★ *Indicates the four specific Domain Elements and nine Indicators that are legislatively mandated.*

Domain	Domain Element	Indicators
Mathematics	Geometry & Spatial Sense	◆ Begins to recognize, describe, compare, and name common shapes, their parts, and attributes. ◆ Progresses in ability to put together and take apart shapes. ◆ Begins to be able to determine whether or not two shapes are the same size and shape. ◆ Shows growth in matching, sorting, putting in a series, and regrouping objects according to one or two attributes such as color, shape, or size. ◆ Builds an increasing understanding of directionality, order, and positions of objects, and words such as up, down, over, under, top, bottom, inside, outside, in front, and behind.
	Patterns & Measurement	◆ Enhances abilities to recognize, duplicate, and extend simple patterns using a variety of materials. ◆ Shows increasing abilities to match, sort, put in a series, and regroup objects according to one or two attributes such as shape or size. ◆ Begins to make comparisons between several objects based on a single attribute. ◆ Shows progress in using standard and non-standard measures for length and area of objects.
Science	Scientific Skills & Methods	◆ Begins to use senses and a variety of tools and simple measuring devices to gather information, investigate materials, and observe processes and relationships. ◆ Develops increased ability to observe and discuss common properties, differences, and comparisons among objects and materials. ◆ Begins to participate in simple investigations to test observations, discuss and draw conclusions, and form generalizations. ◆ Develops growing abilities to collect, describe, and record information through a variety of means, including discussion, drawings, maps, and charts. ◆ Begins to describe and discuss predictions, explanations, and generalizations based on past experiences.

★ *Indicates the four specific Domain Elements and nine Indicators that are legislatively mandated.*

Domain	Domain Element	Indicators
Science	Scientific Knowledge	◆ Expands knowledge of and abilities to observe, describe, and discuss the natural world, materials, living things, and natural processes. ◆ Expands knowledge of and respect for their bodies and the environment. ◆ Develops growing awareness of ideas and language related to attributes of time and temperature. ◆ Shows increased awareness and beginning understanding of changes in materials and cause-effect relationships.
Creative Arts	Music	◆ Participates with increasing interest and enjoyment in a variety of music activities, including listening, singing, finger-plays, games, and performances. ◆ Experiments with a variety of musical instruments.
	Art	◆ Gains ability in using different art media and materials in a variety of ways for creative expression and representation. ◆ Progresses in abilities to create drawings, paintings, models, and other art creations that are more detailed, creative, or realistic. ◆ Develops growing abilities to plan, work independently, and demonstrate care and persistence in a variety of art projects. ◆ Begins to understand and share opinions about artistic products and experiences.
	Movement	◆ Expresses through movement and dancing what is felt and heard in various musical tempos and styles. ◆ Shows growth in moving in time to different patterns of beat and rhythm in music.
	Dramatic Play	◆ Participates in a variety of dramatic play activities that become more extended and complex. ◆ Shows growing creativity and imagination in using materials and in assuming different roles in dramatic play situations.

★ Indicates the four specific Domain Elements and nine Indicators that are legislatively mandated.

Domain	Domain Element	Indicators
Social & Emotional Development	Self-Concept	◆ Begins to develop and express awareness of self in terms of specific abilities, characteristics, and preferences. ◆ Develops growing capacity for independence in a range of activities, routines, and tasks. ◆ Demonstrates growing confidence in a range of abilities and expresses pride in accomplishments.
	Self-Control	◆ Shows progress in expressing feelings, needs, and opinions in difficult situations and conflicts without harming themselves, others, or property. ◆ Develops growing understanding of how their actions affect others and begins to accept the consequences of their actions. ◆ Demonstrates increasing capacity to follow rules and routines and use materials purposefully, safely, and respectfully.
	Cooperation	◆ Increases abilities to sustain interactions with peers by helping, sharing, and discussion. ◆ Shows increasing abilities to use compromise and discussion in working, playing, and resolving conflicts with peers. ◆ Develops increasing abilities to give and take in interactions; to take turns in games or using materials; and to interact without being overly submissive or directive.
	Social Relationships	◆ Demonstrates increasing comfort in talking with and accepting guidance and directions from a range of familiar adults. ◆ Shows progress in developing friendships with peers. ◆ Progresses in responding sympathetically to peers who are in need, upset, hurt, or angry; and in expressing empathy or caring for others.
	Knowledge of Families & Communities	◆ Develops ability to identify personal characteristics including gender and family composition. ◆ Progresses in understanding similarities and respecting differences among people, such as genders, race, special needs, culture, language, and family structures. ◆ Develops growing awareness of jobs and what is required to perform them. ◆ Begins to express and understand concepts and language of geography in the contexts of their classroom, home, and community.

★ *Indicates the four specific Domain Elements and nine Indicators that are legislatively mandated.*

Domain	Domain Element	Indicators
Approaches to Learning	Initiative & Curiosity	◆ Chooses to participate in an increasing variety of tasks and activities. ◆ Develops increased ability to make independent choices. ◆ Approaches tasks and activities with increased flexibility, imagination, and inventiveness. ◆ Grows in eagerness to learn about and discuss a growing range of topics, ideas, and tasks.
	Engagement & Persistence	◆ Grows in abilities to persist in and complete a variety of tasks, activities, projects, and experiences. ◆ Demonstrates increasing ability to set goals and develop and follow through on plans. ◆ Shows growing capacity to maintain concentration over time on a task, question, set of directions or interactions, despite distractions and interruptions.
	Reasoning & Problem Solving	◆ Develops increasing ability to find more than one solution to a question, task, or problem. ◆ Grows in recognizing and solving problems through active exploration, including trial and error, and interactions and discussions with peers and adults. ◆ Develops increasing abilities to classify, compare, and contrast objects, events, and experiences.
Physical Health & Development	Gross Motor Skills	◆ Shows increasing levels of proficiency, control, and balance in walking, climbing, running, jumping, hopping, skipping, marching, and galloping. ◆ Demonstrates increasing abilities to coordinate movements in throwing, catching, kicking, bouncing balls, and using the slide and swing.
	Fine Motor Skills	◆ Develops growing strength, dexterity, and control needed to use tools such as scissors, paper punch, stapler, and hammer. ◆ Grows in hand-eye coordination in building with blocks, putting together puzzles, reproducing shapes and patterns, stringing beads, and using scissors. ◆ Progresses in abilities to use writing, drawing, and art tools, including pencils, markers, chalk, paint brushes, and various types of technology.

★ *Indicates the four specific Domain Elements and nine Indicators that are legislatively mandated.*

Domain	Domain Element	Indicators
Physical Health & Development	Health Status & Practices	◆ Progresses in physical growth, strength, stamina, and flexibility. ◆ Participates actively in games, outdoor play, and other forms of exercise that enhance physical fitness. ◆ Shows growing independence in hygiene, nutrition, and personal care when eating, dressing, washing hands, brushing teeth, and toileting. ◆ Builds awareness and ability to follow basic health and safety rules such as fire safety, traffic and pedestrian safety, and responding appropriately to potentially harmful objects, substances, and activities.
★ *Indicates the four specific Domain Elements and nine Indicators that are legislatively mandated.*		

Appendix D: Head Start and High/Scope Alignments

Aligning Child Observation Record (COR) Items With Head Start Domains and Child Outcome Elements/Indicators

Aligned COR Items	Head Start Domain	Domain Element	Require Head Start Child Outcome Indicators
A. Making choices and plans H. Understanding and expressing feelings Q. Listening to and understanding speech R. Using vocabulary S. Using complex patterns of speech CC. Identifying position and direction DD. Identifying sequence, change, and causality	1. Language Development	Listening & Understanding	★ Understands an increasingly complex and varied vocabulary. ★ For non-English-speaking children, progresses in listening to and understanding English.
		Speaking & Communicating	★ Develops increasing abilities to understand and use language to communicate information, experiences, ideas, feelings, opinions, needs, questions, and for other varied purposes. ★ Uses an increasingly complex and varied spoken vocabulary. ★ For non-English-speaking children, progresses in speaking English.

Aligned COR Items	Head Start Domain	Domain Element	Require Head Start Child Outcome Indicators
T. Showing awareness of sounds in words U. Demonstrating knowledge about books V. Using letter names and sounds W. Reading X. Writing	2. Literacy	★ Phonological Awareness (T, V, X)	★ Associates sounds with written words, such as awareness that different words begin with the same sound.
		★ Book Knowledge & Appreciation (U)	*All Indicators for Book Knowledge & Appreciation are mandated.*
		★ Print Awareness & Concepts (U, V, W, X)	★ Recognizes a word as a unit of print, or awareness that letters are grouped to form words, and that words are separated by spaces.
		Early Writing	
		Alphabet Knowledge	★ Identifies at least 10 letters of the alphabet, especially those in their own name. ★ Knows that letters of the alphabet are a special category of visual graphics that can be individually named.
Y. Sorting objects Z. Identifying patterns AA. Comparing properties BB. Counting CC. Identifying position and direction	3. Mathematics	★ Number & Operations	*All Indicators for Number & Operations are mandated.*
		Geometry & Spatial Sense	
		Patterns & Measurement	
Y. Sorting objects AA. Comparing properties DD. Identifying sequence, change, and causality EE. Identifying materials and properties FF. Identifying natural and living things	4. Science	Scientific Skills & Methods	
		Scientific Knowledge	

Aligned COR Items	Head Start Domain	Domain Element	Required Head Start Child Outcome Indicators
I. Making and building models J. Drawing and painting pictures K. Pretending O. Moving to music P. Singing	5. Creative Arts	Music Art Movement Dramatic Play	
E. Relating to adults F. Relating to other children G. Resolving interpersonal conflict H. Understanding and expressing feelings	6. Social & Emotional Development	Self-Concept Self-Control Cooperation Social Relationships Knowledge of Families & Communities	
A. Making choices and plans B. Solving problems with materials C. Initiating play D. Taking care of personal needs	7. Approaches to Learning	Initiative & Curiosity Engagement & Persistence Reasoning & Problem Solving	
D. Taking care of personal needs L. Moving in various ways M. Moving with objects N. Feeling and expressing steady beat	8. Physical Health & Development	Fine Motor Skills Gross Motor Skills Health Status & Practices	

★ Legislatively mandated Domain Elements and Indicators

Note: Letter in parentheses ( ) indicate corresponding COR items.

Aligning the Preschool PQA With Head Start Program Performance Standards

Introduction

The Program Quality Assessment (PQA) is an excellent tool for rating the quality of center-based Head Start programs and identifying the training needs of Head Start staff. Head Start has always aimed to be a national model of "best practices" in early childhood and family service programs. The PQA is also based on the field's commonly held positions about best practices. In fact, the Head Start Program Performance Standards (HSPPS; Federal Register, 1996; U.S. Department of Health and Human Services, 2002) were a primary reference in the development of the instrument. Consequently, the PQA is highly compatible with Head Start program goals and implementation strategies. Because of this alignment, the PQA has been used in a series of studies to evaluate staff qualifications and staff development in Head Start and to assess the relationship between program quality and Head Start's effectiveness in promoting children's development (e.g., Epstein, 1993, 1999; Schweinhart, 2000; Schweinhart, Epstein, Okoloko, & Oden, 1998; Schweinhart, Oden, Okoloko, Epstein, & Markley, 2000). These studies are described in the section on "Psychometric Properties" in the PQA Administration Manual.

Like Head Start, the PQA focuses comprehensively on children's learning experiences, parent involvement and family services, staff development, and overall program management. Whether administered as a self-assessment or by a trained outside rater, the PQA can help Head Start programs identify and achieve optimum levels of quality in all these areas. The PQA provides Head Start programs with meaningful data as they conduct required self-assessments, prepare for onsite program reviews, develop plans for staff training and program development, and generally monitor and strive to improve the quality of their services. Moreover, unlike many compliance measures that score programs according to a simple yes-no dichotomy, the PQA measures quality along a five-point continuum. It clearly defines, in measurable terms, the conditions and practices that constitute low, moderate, and high quality implementation. This range allows Head Start programs to pinpoint their current status and their chart progress over time.

To maximize the usefulness of the PQA to Head Start programs, High/Scope has prepared this Head Start guide to the PQA. The guide maps the relationship between the PQA and the HSPPS. Many PQA items address more than one standard.

The Standards covered in whole or in part by the PQA are Definitions (1304.03), Child Health and Developmental Services (1304.20), Education and Early Childhood Development (1304.21), Child Health and Safety (1304.22), Child Nutrition (1304.23), Child Mental Health (1304.24), Family Partnerships (1304.40), Community Partnerships (1304.41), Program Governance (1304.50), Management Systems and Procedures (1304.51), Human Resource Management (1304.52), and Facilities, Materials, and Equipment (1304.53). Because the Preschool PQA is designed to assess center-based preschool-age programs in general, the alignment does not include Standards limited to home-based or infant-toddler (Early Head Start) programs, or requirements unique to Head Start's organizational and committee structure.

The following is a listing of the relevant HSPPS followed by an alignment of the PQA items with the Standard(s) addressed by that item.

Adapted from High/Scope Educational Research Foundation, Preschool Program Quality Assessment (PQA), Second Edition (Ypsilanti, MI: High/Scope Press, 2003).

Head Start Program Performance Standards[1] Addressed by the Preschool PQA

HSPPS 1304.03 Definitions

5. The curriculum is consistent with the Head Start Program Performance Standards and is based on sound child development principles about how children grow and learn. Curriculum means a written plan that includes

    i. The goals for children's development and learning

    ii. The experiences through which they will achieve these goals

    iii. What staff and parents do to help children achieve these goals

    iv. The materials needed to support the implementation of the curriculum

HSPPS 1304.20 Child Health and Developmental Services

(a) Determining child health status

    1. Within 90 days of program entry, determine and arrange for ongoing health care.

(b) Developmental, sensory, and behavioral screening

    1. Within 45 days of program entry, conduct screening.

    2. Obtain guidance from appropriate mental health or child development professional.

    3. Use multiple sources of information about child including family, teachers, and other staff.

(c) Extended follow-up and treatment

    1. Establish system on ongoing communication with parents.

    2. Assist parents in enabling medication, equipment, or other child health aids.

    3. Enable prevention and treatment as recommended by dental professional.

    4. Provide related services as specified in Individualized Education Plan (IEP) and Individualized Family Service Plan (IFSP).

(d) Ongoing care — Agencies must implement ongoing procedures (including observations from parents and staff) to identify new or recurring medical, dental, or developmental concerns so they can make appropriate referrals.

(e) Involving parents — Agencies must

    1. Consult with parents immediately when problems are suspected or identified.

    2. Explain diagnostic/testing procedures and results to parents.

    3. Talk to parents about how to familiarize children with medical procedures.

    4. Assist parents to enroll in system of ongoing family health care.

(f) Individualization of the program

    1. Agencies must use information from testing and parental/staff input to determine how to best respond to child's individual needs.

HSPPS 1304.21 Education and Early Childhood Development

(a) Child development and education approach for all children

    1. To help children be prepared to succeed in their present environment and later responsibilities in school and life, agencies must

---

[1]Many of the Standards are quoted verbatim. However, for clarity and brevity, some items have been reworded or condensed, without changing the essence of the item.

i.   Be developmentally and linguistically appropriate.

ii. Be inclusive of children with disabilities.

iii. Support and respect gender, culture, language, ethnicity, and family composition.

iv. Provide daily balance of child-initiated and adult-directed activities, including individual and small-group activities.

v.   Allow and enable children to independently use toilet facilities.

2. Parents must be

i.   Invited to become integrally involved in the development of the program's curriculum and educational approach

ii. Provided with opportunities to increase child observational skills and share their assessments with staff

iii. Encouraged to participate in staff-parent conferences and home visits to discuss child's development and education

3. Agencies must support social and emotional development by

i.   Enhancing child's strengths by

A. Building trust

B. Fostering independence

C. Encouraging self-control by setting clear, consistent limits and having realistic expectations

D. Encouraging respect for the feelings and rights of others

E. Supporting and respecting child's home language, culture, and family composition

ii. Planning for routines and transitions so they occur in a timely and predictable manner

4. Agencies must provide for development of children's cognitive and language skills by

i.   Using various strategies (experimentation, inquiry, observation, play, and exploration) to support learning

ii. Ensuring opportunities for creative expression through such activities as art, music, movement, dialogue

iii. Promoting interaction and language use among children and between children and adults

iv. Supporting emerging literacy and numeracy development

5. Agencies in center-based settings must promote physical development by

i.   Providing sufficient time, indoor and outdoor space, materials and adult guidance for gross motor development

ii. Providing sufficient time, indoor and outdoor space, materials, and adult guidance for fine motor development

(c) Child development and education approach for preschoolers

1. Agencies in collaboration with parents must implement a curriculum that

i.   Supports each child's individual pattern of development and learning

ii. Provides for the development of cognitive skills that form a foundation for school readiness and later school success including age-appropriate literacy, numeracy, reasoning, problem-solving and decision-making skills

iii. Integrates all educational aspects of health, nutrition, and mental health services into program activities

iv. Helps children develop emotional security and facility in social relationships

v. Enhances child's understanding of self as an individual and as a member of a group

vi. Provides opportunities for success to help children develop feelings of competence, self-esteem, and positive attitudes toward learning

vii. Provides individual and small-group experiences both indoors and outdoors

2. Staff must use a variety of strategies to promote learning and development based on observations and ongoing assessment of each child.

HSPPS 1304.22 Child Health and Safety

(a) Health emergency procedures

1. Posted emergency plans

2. Emergency service and family contact information

3. Evacuation routes

4. Parental notification procedures

5. Methods for handling/reporting child abuse and neglect

(b) Conditions of short-term exclusion and admittance

1. Agencies must temporarily exclude a child with short-term injury or contagious illness that cannot be readily accommodated in center-based programs if it imposes health or safety risk to child or others.

2. Agencies may not exclude child on long-term basis based on health care needs or medical requirements unless it poses a significant hazard.

3. Agencies must request that parents inform them of health or safety needs of child; must share necessary information with staff in accordance with program's confidentiality policy.

(c) Medication administration

1. Labeling and storing

2. Administering

3. Written instructions and authorization

4. Maintaining individual records

(d) Injury prevention

1. Agencies must ensure that staff and volunteers can demonstrate safety practices.

2. Foster safety awareness among children and parents through appropriate program activities.

(e) Hygiene

1. Staff, volunteers, and children must wash hands with soap and running water at following times:

i. Diapering and toilet use

ii. Food preparation and consumption

iii. When hands contaminated with bodily fluids

iv. After handling animals and pets

2. Staff, volunteers, and children must wash hands with soap and running water at following times:

i. Before and after giving medication

ii. Before and after treating injuries

iii. After assisting children with toileting

3. Use of nonporous latex gloves

4. Cleaning spills of bodily fluids

(f) First-aid kits

   1. Readily available and well-supplied, accessible to staff but out of children's reach

   2. Restocked after use; conduct inventory at regular intervals

HSPPS 1304.23 Child Nutrition

(a) Identification of individual, family, community, or cultural nutritional needs and practices

(b) Nutritional services

   1. Programs must meet nutritional and feeding needs of children and consider cultural/ethnic preferences.

     ii. Children in part-day centers must receive snacks and meals that meet nutritional needs.

     v. Serving sizes and content must meet USDA guidelines.

     vi. Food must be high in nutrition and low in fat, sugar, and salt.

   3. Staff must promote effective dental hygiene in conjunction with meals.

(c) Meal service — Agencies must contribute to socialization of children by providing that

   1. A variety of food is served to broaden children's food experiences.

   2. Food is not used as a punishment or reward.

   3. Sufficient time is allowed for each child to eat.

   4. Eating is family style for preschoolers and staff.

   6. Medically based diets or other dietary requirements are accommodated.

7. Children are involved in food-related activities as developmentally appropriate.

(e) Food safety and sanitation

   1. Compliance with licensing requirements

HSPPS 1304.24 Child Mental Health

(a) Mental health services

   1. Agencies must work collaboratively with parents by

     i. Soliciting parental information, observations, concerns about their child's health

     ii. Sharing staff observations with parents and information about separation and attachment issues

     iii. Discussing with parents appropriate responses to their children's behavior

     iv. Discussing how to strengthen nurturing environments at home and in the program

     v. Helping parents better understand mental health issues

     vi. Supporting parental involvement in mental health interventions

   2. Utilize on-site or referrals to community mental health services as needed.

HSPPS 1304.40 Family Partnerships

(a) Family goal setting

   1. Referrals to community services as needed

   4. Variety of opportunities for interaction with parents throughout the year

   5. Meetings and interactions respectful of family diversity

(b) Accessing community services and resources

1. Agencies must work with families to access services and resources that include

    i. Emergency/crisis assistance in food, housing, clothing, transportation

    ii. Education and counseling programs on child abuse/neglect, substance abuse, domestic violence

    iii. Continuing education and employment training

(d) Parent involvement — general

1. Agencies must provide opportunities in policy making, parent involvement, and education.

2. Program settings must be open to parents during all program hours; parents must be welcomed; all parent participation must be voluntary and not a requirement for child's enrollment.

3. Agencies must provide parents with opportunities to participate in the program as employees or volunteers.

(e) Parent involvement in child development and education

1. Agencies must include parents in the development of the curriculum and approach to child development.

3. Agencies must provide opportunities for parents to enhance their parenting skills and understanding of child development.

5. Center-based programs must conduct two home visits and at least two staff-parent conferences per year.

(f) Parent involvement in health, nutrition, and mental health education

1. Agencies must provide education programs in health (medical and dental), nutrition, and mental health.

(g) Parent involvement in community advocacy

1. Agencies must

    i. Support and encourage parents to make community services responsive to their needs

    ii. Establish procedures to provide parents with comprehensive information about community resources

2. Parents must be provided with regular opportunities to work together on activities of interest to them.

(h) Parent involvement in transition activities

1. Agencies must assist parents in becoming their child's advocate as they transition into the program from home or another child care setting, and from the program to another preschool, child care setting, or elementary school.

(i) Parent involvement in home visits

2. Teachers in center-based programs must make at least two visits per year to home of enrolled children (unless parent does not permit it).

3. Home visits must be scheduled at times mutually convenient for families and staff.

4. Visits may take place at the program site or another safe location that affords privacy.

HSPPS 1304.41 Community Partnerships

(a) Partnerships

2. Agencies must take affirmative steps with community agencies to support responsiveness to child and family needs.

(c) Transition services

    1. Agencies must establish procedures with child care/school/other agencies to support successful transitions including

        i. Coordination for transfer of records

        ii. Outreach to encourage communication among all relevant staff

        iii. Initiating meetings between parents and teachers

        iv. Initiating joint transition-related activities

HSPPS 1304.50 Program Governance

(b) Policy group composition and formation

    7. Parents of enrolled children must be proportionally represented on established policy groups.

(d) Policy group responsibilities including

    1. Meeting with management to review following procedures:

        iv. Setting programs goals

        vii. Defining recruitment, selection, and enrollment criteria

        viii. Annual program self-assessment

        ix. Program personnel policies and standards of conduct

        x. Hiring and firing director

        xi. Hiring and firing other staff

(e) Parent committee must carry out at least the following minimal responsibilities

    1. Advise staff in developing and implementing local policies and activities.

    2. Plan, conduct, and participate in formal and informal activities for parents and staff.

    3. Participate in recruitment and screening of employees according to established policies.

HSPPS 1304.51 Management Systems and Procedures

(a) Program planning

    1. Agencies must develop a systematic process of ongoing planning.

(b) General communication — Agencies must share information in a timely manner with parents, policy groups, staff, and the community.

(c) Communication with families

    1. Agencies must ensure effective and regular two-way communication between staff and parents.

(e) Communication among staff — Agencies must have a mechanism for communication among staff to facilitate quality outcomes for children and families.

(g) Record-keeping systems — Agencies must establish and maintain record-keeping systems to provide timely, accurate information and to ensure appropriate confidentiality of this information.

(i) Program self-assessment and monitoring

    1. At least once each year, agencies must conduct a self-assessment.

HSPPS 1304.52 Human Resource Management

(a) Organizational structure

    1. Agencies must establish and maintain an organizational structure that addresses responsibilities assigned to each staff position and provide evidence of adequate mechanisms for staff supervision and support.

(b) Staff qualifications — General

    1. Agencies must ensure that staff and consultants have knowledge, skills, and experiences needed to perform assigned functions.

4. Staff and program consultants must be familiar with ethnic background and heritage of families in programs and be able to communicate, to the extent feasible, with children and families with limited English proficiency.

(c) Head Start director qualifications — Director must have demonstrated skills and abilities in a management capacity relevant to human services program management.

(g) Classroom staffing and home visitors — Agencies must meet requirements regarding

   1. Child-staff ratios

   3. Group size

(h) Standards of conduct

   1. Agencies must ensure that staff, consultants, and volunteers abide by standards of conduct that specify

     i. They will respect and promote the unique identity of each child and family and refrain from stereotyping on the basis of gender, race, ethnicity, culture, religion, or disability.

     ii. They will follow the program's confidentiality policies.

     iii. No child will be left alone or unsupervised while under their care.

     iv. They will use positive methods of child guidance and will not engage in corporal punishment, emotional or physical abuse, or humiliation; they will not employ discipline methods involving isolation, use of food as punishment or reward, or denial of basic needs.

3. Personnel policies must include provision of penalties for violating standards of conduct.

(i) Staff performance appraisals — Agencies must at a minimum perform annual performance reviews for staff members and use results to identify staff training and professional development needs and assist each staff member in improving his/her skills and professional competencies.

(j) Staff and volunteer health — Agencies must ensure that each staff member and volunteer has an initial health and screening examination.

(k) Training and development

   1. Agencies must provide an orientation to all new staff, consultants, and volunteers that includes at minimum goals and philosophy of Head Start and ways in which they are implemented by the program.

   2. Agencies must implement a structured approach to staff training and development, attaching academic credit whenever possible; this system should be designed to help build relationships among staff and assist staff in acquiring and increasing knowledge and skills needed to fulfill their job responsibilities.

   3. Training must include information on reporting child abuse, helping families transition to/from Head Start.

HSPPS 1304.53 Facilities, Materials, and Equipment

(a) Head Start physical environment and facilities

   1. Agencies must provide a physical environment and facilities conducive to learning and reflective of different stages of children's development.

2. Agencies must provide appropriate space for conduct of all program activities.

3. Center space must be organized into functional areas that can be recognized by children and that allow for individual activities and social interactions.

5. Centers must have at least 35 sq. ft. of usable indoor space and 75 sq. ft. of usable outdoor space per child.

6. Facilities must meet licensing requirements.

7. Agencies must provide for maintenance, repair, safety, and security of all facilities, materials, and equipment.

8. Agencies must provide a center-based environment free of toxins.

9. Outdoor play areas must be arranged to prevent children from leaving premises; no unsupervised exposure to traffic areas en route to/from program.

10. Agencies must conduct safety inspections at least annually regarding space, light, ventilation, heat, and other physical arrangements consistent with children's health and safety needs.

(b) Head Start equipment, toys, materials, and furniture

1. Agencies must provide/arrange sufficient equipment, toys, materials, and furniture to facilitate participation of children and adult. Must be

   i. Supportive of specific educational objectives of local program

   ii. Supportive of cultural and ethnic backgrounds of children

   iii. Age-appropriate, safe, and supportive of abilities and developmental level of each child, with necessary adaptation for children with disabilities

   iv. Accessible, attractive, and inviting to children

   v. Designed to provide a variety of learning experiences and encourage each child to experiment and explore

   vi. Safe, durable, and kept in good condition

   vii. Stored in safe and orderly fashion when not in use

How PQA Items Align With the Head Start Program Performance Standards

Preschool PQA Item	Relevant Head Start Program Performance Standards
I. Learning Environment	
A. Safe and healthy environment	1304.22 (a, d, e, f), 1304.23 (e), 1304.53 (a, b)
B. Defined interest areas	1304.53 (a)
C. Logically located interest areas	1304.53 (a)
D. Outdoor space, equipment, materials	1304.21 (a, c), 1304.53 (a)
E. Organization and labeling of materials	1304.21 (a, c), 1304.53 (b)
F. Varied and open-ended materials	1304.21 (a, c), 1304.53 (b)
G. Plentiful materials	1304.21 (a, c), 1304.53 (b)
H. Diversity-related materials	1304.21 (a), 1304.23 (a), 1304.40 (a), 1304.53 (b)
I. Displays of child-initiated work	1304.21 (a, c)
II. Daily Routine	
A. Consistent daily routine	1304.21 (a, c)
B. Parts of the day	1304.21 (a, c)
C. Appropriate time for each part of day	1304.21 (a, c)
D. Time for child planning	1304.21 (a, c)
E. Time for child-initiated activities	1304.21 (a, c)
F. Time for child recall	1304.21 (a, c)
G. Small-group time	1304.21 (a, c)
H. Large-group time	1304.21 (a, c)
I. Choices during transition times	1304.21 (a, c)
J. Cleanup with reasonable choices	1304.21 (a, c)
K. Snack or meal time	1304.21 (a, c), 1304.23 (c)
L. Outside time	1304.21 (a, c)
III. Adult-Child Interaction	
A. Meeting basic physical needs	1304.21 (a, c), 1304.23 (b, c), 1304.52 (h)
B. Handling separation from home	1304.21 (a, c), 1304.24 (a), 1304.40 (e)
C. Warm and caring atmosphere	1304.21 (a, c), 1304.52 (h)
D. Support for child communication	1304.21 (a, c)
E. Support for non-English speakers	1304.21 (a, c), 1304.52 (b, g)
F. Adults as partners in play	1304.21 (a, c)
G. Encouragement of child initiatives	1304.21 (a, c)
H. Support for learning at group times	1304.21 (a, c)
I. Opportunities for child explorations	1304.21 (a, c)
J. Acknowledgment of child efforts	1304.21 (a, c)
K. Encouragement for peer interactions	1304.21 (a, c)
L. Independent problem solving	1304.21 (a, c)
M. Conflict resolution	1304.21 (a, c)

(Continued on next page)

Preschool PQA Item	Relevant Head Start Program Performance Standards
IV. Curriculum Planning and Assessment	
A. Curriculum model	1304.03 (5), 1304.21 (a, c), 1304.51 (a)
B. Team teaching	1304.51 (e), 1304.52 (g)
C. Comprehensive child records	1304.51 (g)
D. Anecdotal note taking by staff	1304.21 (a, c)
E. Use of child observation measure	1304.21 (a, c)
V. Parent Involvement and Family Services	
A. Opportunities for involvement	1304.21 (a), 1304.40 (a, d–i)
B. Parents on policy-making committees	1304.40 (d), 1304.50 (b, e)
C. Parent participation in child activities	1304.21 (a), 1304.40 (d, e), 1304.51 (c)
D. Sharing of curriculum information	1304.21 (a), 1304.40 (d, e), 1304.51 (b, c)
E. Staff-parent informal interactions	1304.21 (a), 1304.40 (d, e) ,1304.51 (c)
F. Extending learning at home	1304.21 (a), 1304.40 (d, e), 1304.51 (c)
G. Formal meetings with parents	1304.21 (a), 1304.40 (d, e, i), 1304.51 (c)
H. Diagnostic/special education services	1304.20 (a–f), 1304.24 (a)
I. Service referrals as needed	1304.24 (a), 1304.40 (a, b), 1304.41 (a)
J. Transition to kindergarten	1304.40 (h), 1304.41 (c)
VI. Staff Qualifications and Staff Development	
A. Program director background	1304.52 (a, b, c)
B. Instructional staff background	1304.52 (b, g)
C. Support staff orientation & supervision	1304.52 (i, j)
D. Ongoing professional development	1304.52 (k)
E. Inservice training content and methods	1304.52 (k)
F. Observation and feedback	1304.52 (a, i)
G. Professional organization affiliation	1304.52 (k)
VII. Program Management	
A. Program licensed	1304.22 (a–f), 1304.23 (e), 1304.52 (j), 1304.53 (a, b)
B. Continuity in instructional staff	1304.52 (g)
C. Program assessment	1304.50 (d), 1304.51 (i), 1304.52 (k)
D. Recruitment and enrollment plan	1304.40 (h), 1304.50 (d), 1304.51 (a)
E. Operating policies and procedures	1304.22 (a–d), 1304.50 (d), 1304.51 (g), 1304.52 (h, k)
F. Accessibility for those with disabilities	1304.21 (a), 1304.53 (a)
G. Adequacy of program funding	1304.40 (d–i) ,1304.52 (b), 1304.52 (k), 1304.53 (a, b)

References

Epstein, A. S. (1993). *Training for quality: Improving early childhood programs through systematic inservice training.* Ypsilanti, MI: High/Scope Press.

Epstein, A. S. (1999). Pathways to quality in Head Start, public school, and private non-profit early childhood programs. *Journal of Research in Childhood Education, 13*(2), 101–119.

Federal Register (1996, November 05). *Program Performance Standards for the operation of Head Start programs by grantee and delegate agencies.* Washington, DC: U.S. Government Printing Office, 57210–57227.

Schweinhart, L. J. (2000, June). *Hansel Head Start program quality: A report to the Community Foundation of St. Joseph.* Ypsilanti, MI: High/Scope Educational Research Foundation, Research Division.

Schweinhart, L. J., Epstein, A. S., Okoloko, V., & Oden, S. (1998, July). *How staffing and staff development contribute to Head Start program quality and effectiveness.* Paper presented at the Head Start Quality Research Center Consortium Poster Symposium, Head Start Fourth National Research Conference, Washington, DC.

Schweinhart, L. J., Oden, S., Okoloko, V., Epstein, A. S., & Markley, C. (2000, June). *Early results: Implementation of a Head Start effectiveness study using random assignment.* Poster session presented at the Head Start Fifth National Research Conference, Washington, DC.

U.S. Department of Health and Human Services, Administration for Children and Families, Head Start Bureau. (2002, October). *Program Performance Standards and other regulations.* http://www2.acf.dhhs.gov/programs/hsb/performance/index.htm

References

Burts, D. C., Hart, C. H., Charlesworth, R. Fleege, P. O., Mosley, J., & Thomasson, R. H. (1992). Observed activities and stress behaviors of children in developmentally appropriate and inappropriate kindergarten classrooms. *Early Childhood Research Quarterly, 7,* 297–318.

Center for Law and Social Policy. (n.d.). *Cost of meeting House and Senate proposed Head Start teacher qualifications.* Retrieved December 19, 2007, from http://www.clasp.org/publications/head_start_memo.pdf

Daniels, M. (2000). *Dancing with words: Signing for hearing children's literacy.* Westport, CT: Bergin & Garvey.

DeBruin-Parecki, A. (2004). *Early Literacy Skills Assessment user guide.* Ypsilanti, MI: High/Scope Press.

DeBruin-Parecki, A., & Hohmann, M. (2003). *Letter links: Alphabet learning with children's names.* Ypsilanti, MI: High/Scope Press.

DHHS. *See* U.S. Department of Health and Human Services.

Epstein, A. S. (1993). *Training for quality: Improving early childhood programs through systematic inservice training.* Ypsilanti, MI: High/Scope Press.

Epstein, A. S. (2003). All about High/Scope. *High/Scope ReSource: A Magazine for Educators, 22*(1), 5–7.

Epstein, A. S. (2006). High/Scope and Head Start: A good fit. *High/Scope ReSource: A Magazine for Educators, 25*(1), 5–12.

Epstein, A. S. (2007). *Essentials of active learning in preschool: Getting to know the High/Scope Curriculum.* Ypsilanti, MI: High/Scope Press.

Glod, M. (2007, November 15). Bill to expand Head Start, bolster its teacher qualifications is approved. *The Washington Post.* p. A8.

Hart, B., & Risley, T. R. (1995). *Meaningful differences in the everyday experiences of young American children.* Baltimore: Paul H. Brookes.

Head Start English Language Learners Project. (n.d.). *What is an ELL?* Retrieved November 19, 2007, from http://www.hellp.org/about/ell.asp

Head Start Program Performance Standards and Other Regulations, 44 C.F.R.§1301–1311 (2006).

High/Scope Educational Research Foundation. (2003a). *Preschool Child Observation Record (COR), Second edition.* Ypsilanti, MI: High/Scope Press.

High/Scope Educational Research Foundation. (2003b). *Preschool Program Quality Assessment (PQA), Second edition.* Ypsilanti, MI: High/Scope Press.

High/Scope Educational Research Foundation. (2004). *Early Literacy Skills Assessment (ELSA).* Ypsilanti, MI: HIgh/Scope Press.

High/Scope Educational Research Foundation. (2005). *Growing Readers Early Literacy Curriculum (GRC).* Ypsilanti, MI: High/Scope Press.

Hohmann, M., Weikart, D. P., & Epstein, A. S. (2008). *Educating young children: Active learning practices for preschool and child care programs* (3rd ed.). Ypsilanti, MI: High/Scope Press.

HSPPS. *See* Head Start Program Performance Standards.

Kohn, A. (1999). *Punished by rewards: The trouble with gold stars, incentive plans, A's, praise, and other bribes.* New York: Houghton Mifflin.

Marcon, R. (2002). Moving up the grades: Relationship between preschool model and later school success. *Early Childhood Research and Practice, 4*(1). Retrieved December 6, 2007, from http://ecrp.uiuc.edu/v4nl/marcon.html

National Head Start Association. (2006). *Keeping Head Start funding federal to local* (Issue Brief). Alexandria, VA: National Head Start Association. Retrieved December 11, 2007, from http://www.nhsa.org/download/advocacy/fact/HSFund.pdf

Reynolds, A. J., Temple, J. A., Robertson, D. L., & Mann, E. A. (2001). Long-term effects of an early childhood intervention on educational achievement and juvenile arrest: A 15-year follow-up of low-income children in public schools. *Journal of the American Medical Association, 285,* 2339–2346.

Schweinhart, L. J., Montie, J., Xiang, Z., Barnett, W. S., Belfield, C. R., & Nores, M. (2005). *Lifetime effects: The High/Scope Perry Preschool Study through age 40.* Ypsilanti, MI: High/Scope Press.

Schweinhart, L. J., Weikart, D. P., & Larner, M. B. (1986). *Consequences of three preschool curriculum models through age 15.* Ypsilanti, MI: High/Scope Press.

U.S. Department of Health and Human Services, Administration for Children and Families. (2002). *Head Start early literacy training* (Administration on Children, Youth and Families Information Memorandum). Washington, DC: U.S. Department of Health and Human Services.

U.S. Department of Health and Human Services, Administration for Children and Families. (2003). *The Head Start path to positive child outcomes.* Retrieved January 31, 2008, from http://www.hsnrc.org/CDI/pdfs/hsoutcomespath28ppREV.pdf

U.S. Department of Health and Human Services, Administration for Children and Families. (2007a). *Head Start program fact sheet: Fiscal year 2007.* Washington, DC: U.S. Department of Health and Human Services.

U.S. Department of Health and Human Services, Administration for Children and Families. (2007b). *The Healthy Marriage Initiative.* Retrieved December 11, 2007, from http://www.acf.hhs.gov/healthymarriage/about/mission.html#background

Zigler, E., & Muenchow, S. (1992). *Head Start: The inside story of America's most successful educational experiment.* New York: Basic Books.

Zill, N., Resnick, G., & Kim, K., O'Donnell, K., Sorongon, A. (2003). *Head Start FACES 2000: A whole-child perspective on program performance, Fourth progress report.* Washington, DC: U.S. Department of Health and Human Services.

Index

About the Author

Karen "Kay" Rush is an Early Childhood Specialist at the High/Scope Educational Research Foundation in Ypsilanti, Michigan, where she trains and mentors preschool teachers in the High/Scope Curriculum and writes articles for High/Scope's publications, *ReSource* and *Extensions*. Kay also serves as a substitute teacher at the High/Scope Demonstration Preschool.

Before joining High/Scope, Kay worked her way up through the ranks of Head Start, beginning, in 1981, as an assistant teacher and progressing to teacher, center administrator, assistant education coordinator, and education coordinator. She holds a bachelor's degree in sign language studies and a master's degree in early childhood education. A licensed minister, Kay is the founder and director of Lift Up Your Hands Ministries, where she directs a community sign-mime choir that ministers to hearing and Deaf audiences using American Sign Language and pantomime with Gospel, Christian, and inspirational music. It was at High/Scope where Kay joined her two passions together (early childhood and sign language) to develop workshops and seminars to help preschool teachers enhance children's literacy skills through sign language.

Kay resides in Belleville, Michigan, with her husband, with whom she co-owns Rush Travels & Adventures, a travel and trip planning business. She is the very proud mother of three beautiful grown children, Marlon, Tommie, and SharRon, and the very proud grandmother of Tommie Rush V and his older sister, Naptyla, who both affectionately call her "Grammy Kay."